PRAISE FOR *GILDED*

"With *Gilded*, Keren offers a profound and much-needed reflection on the pressures of ambition and success, pulling back the curtain on the gilded cage we build around ourselves. This book provides not just inspiration but the tools to truly break free and redefine what success means, on your own terms."

—Lydia Fenet, author of *The Most Powerful Woman in the Room Is You* and *Claim Your Confidence*

"In *Gilded*, Keren Eldad offers an empowering exploration of the overachiever's paradox—how success, when pursued without alignment, can lead to burnout and emptiness. Through personal anecdotes and practical exercises, she challenges readers to look beyond external markers of success and reconnect with their authentic selves. Her message is a much-needed reminder to shift our focus from external achievements to internal fulfillment, and she provides practical tools for cultivating true joy and purpose. Eldad's wisdom is a gift for anyone who feels trapped by the relentless pursuit of more."

—Ellen Vora, MD, holistic psychiatrist and author of *The Anatomy of Anxiety*

"In *Gilded*, Keren Eldad brilliantly illuminates a way out of the ambition trap. This book offers a refreshing perspective on success and happiness, providing practical tools to transform burnout into lasting joy and fulfillment."

—Jon Gordon, seventeen-times bestselling author of *The One Truth*

"Keren Eldad, with her deep experience working with high achievers, understands the unique pressures of privilege and overachievement. In *Gilded*, she masterfully reveals the path to escaping the ambition trap, guiding readers toward the ultimate goals of freedom and authenticity. With a blend of wit, wisdom, and practical insight, this book offers a refreshing approach to redefining success and provides actionable strategies for reclaiming balance, inner peace, and true fulfillment."

—Dr. Will Cole, bestselling author of *Gut Feelings*

"I highly recommend Keren Eldad's new book, *Gilded*, which comes at a time when many people are struggling with the strictures of ambition and perfectionism. Keren's approach gives readers the power to break free from the trance of pursuing 'more' and celebrate the present moment."

—Gay Hendricks, author of *The Big Leap*

GILDED

GILDED

BREAKING FREE FROM THE CAGE OF AMBITION, PERFECTIONISM, AND THE RELENTLESS PURSUIT OF MORE

KEREN ELDAD

MIAMI

Cover Design: Lucy Giller
Cover Photo/illustration: stock.adobe.com
Headshot Photography: Shanaz Maharaj
Layout & Design: Lucy Giller

Mango Publishing Group
5966 South Dixie Highway, Suite 300
Miami, FL 33143
info@mango.bz

For special orders, quantity sales, course adoptions and corporate sales, please email the publisher at sales@mango.bz. For trade and wholesale sales, please contact Ingram Publisher Services at customer. service@ingramcontent.com or +1.800.509.4887.

Gilded: Breaking Free from the Cage of Ambition, Perfectionism, and the Relentless Pursuit of More

Library of Congress Cataloging-in-Publication number: 2024947275
ISBN: (print) 978-1-68481-757-3, (ebook) 978-1-68481-758-0
BISAC category code: BUS041000, BUSINESS & ECONOMICS / Management

She's only a bird in a gilded cage,
A beautiful sight to see.
You may think she's happy and free from care.
She's not, though she seems to be...

FROM "BIRD IN A GILDED CAGE,"
BY ARTHUR J. LAMB AND HARRY VON TILZER, 1900

To all my clients who were brave enough to embark on the inner journey and transform their lives.
Your joy is my deepest inspiration.

CONTENTS

Watch Out, Superstar

OVERACHIEVER. That word gets such a bad rap, as if achieving too much is somehow a negative thing. And yet, good or bad, when it comes to describing you, it's probably right on the money.

What other word could describe you, really? You're someone who performs beyond expectations, probably first at school, then socially, and definitely professionally. That's you. You've always been that person. Many other people think they're outstanding, but you have evidence that you actually *are*. Not because of some crazy sense of entitlement or outrageous notion of exceptionalism, but because by now, you have a track record that shows, when you want something, you can go out and get it. You're not afraid of the challenge. You revel in it. You, more than anyone around you, are willing to go the distance.

I know that you know this, which makes my proclamation merely another confirmation that you are exceptional. Unique. But what I really want to tell you is that because of this…you are also under attack.

The assailant? You.

Along with all that overachieving usually comes the corresponding anxiety, the pretense, the posturing, the hypocrisy, the lies, the terror of criticism or ridicule, the exhaustion, the overwhelm, and the punishing self-talk of never being good enough. There's also the pressure that comes from repeated success, the fear of never being as good again. Or, even worse, aimlessness and ennui has set in because, on some level, you know it's all a bit of a charade.

The sad truth is that individuals who overachieve tend to set extremely high standards for themselves, yet never feel satisfied with their accomplishments, because they—you—have boxed themselves into a corner. Even if they do great things, they need to do more. It's a never-ending cycle of success and despair because nothing ever feels as good as it should. And because nothing ever feels as good as it should, the only recourse is to double down and make the next success bigger, the next achievement greater. It's *quite* the dilemma.

Chances are you already know this. If you identify as an overachiever—a winner, a perfectionist, a high performer, or even my favorite term, a "superstar"—then you are quite aware by now that despite your outward success, you vacillate between feeling like king of the world one moment and absolutely worthless the next. Yet, instead of investigating why these wild swings keep recurring, and how to reconcile them, you continue to feed the beast by succumbing to the pressure to keep outperforming.

Is it any wonder you never feel fulfilled?

If you are wondering how I know all this, it's because your type is pretty familiar to me. Not only do I coach people like you for a living, I *am* you. I got straight As all through school. I never missed a chance to compete in academic endeavors. I wasn't blessed athletically, but when it came to spelling bees: Watch out! It wasn't even that long ago that I was in the same red-bottomed shoes as you, using them to climb the same social ladders. I had a successful-looking husband. I held a fast-paced, high-paying job where I vied for any and all chances at recognition, promotions, and raises. I lived in an enviable house. I bragged about my elite college education. I had all the external validations in the world. And that perfect life was plastered all over Instagram.

Yet inside the gilded cage of empty success resided all the same things you may be experiencing: aimlessness. Restlessness. Deep insecurity. Real, palpable resentment. Isolation, loneliness, and frustration. Beneath all the glittering ornaments was a rotting foundation. After years of working extremely hard to measure up to what society told me was important, I felt lost, trapped, and ashamed of my own choices. I lived in a paranoia-in-perpetuity state—compromising my self-regard, my ability to experience joy, my relationships, and every single one of my decisions. In fact, I racked up enormous debt to travel like someone who had made it, to pay for that enviable house, and to always look the part. And even though I went to such long distances to attract and befriend the "right" people, amassing hundreds of acquaintances in high places, I don't think I really trusted anyone. How could I? I didn't trust myself.

Even worse, I found myself in a loveless *and* abusive marriage. My quest for achievement and outward success had caused me to abandon my true self for years. I was caught in a trap of my own making.

You may be familiar with this trap, too. There's a constant feeling that you must be the top player. You need to increase your level of achievement to maintain the same level of reward. This obsession with outward standards and keeping up appearances, however, can quickly become a form of indentured servitude, a hall of mirrors, and a real-life cage. In my sad overachiever story, my marriage was the most obvious sign that my life was only good on paper. In reality, that marriage was loveless, sexless, full of disrespect, lies, and abuse. As a result of the despair I felt inside that marriage, I'd spiraled into a state so desolate, a self-betrayal felt so profoundly, that suicide seemed like my only way out. Thankfully, I convinced myself—and him—that divorce would be easier, even if it meant I had to give up everything.

I wanted a clean break, and that's what I got. But immediately following the divorce, I faced the consequences of the compromised life I'd lived, and all the shoddy ways I'd engineered things to accord with my own false and exceptionally high standards. I had no money (I'd spent it all on that house and the clothes, etc.) and was starting from basically zero in my career and in my finances. I continued to feel pretty awful about myself. During the first months of that transition, I would have told you that my main problem was around money, maybe relationships, or perhaps my choice of career. In truth, it was none of the above. It was always me—the way I saw the world and the way I chose to act in response.

At the start of the downfall, of course, I was confident I could just overachieve my way out of the mess, like I had done every time before. Only this time I found that I couldn't. In very short order, I suffered one devastating blow after another. First, I left my job and moved from Zurich back to New York City, hoping that, once I was home, all would be well. Instead, I met a prolonged struggle to find a new job, which, now that I was broke, only exacerbated this period of deep uncertainty. I moved myself and my two cats onto a kind friend's couch, and my belongings into storage, hoping to "buy time." Then that storage caught fire, and all my belongings—all the clothes, all the accouterments for which I had sacrificed any semblance of financial wellbeing—burned to the ground. And then, both my cats died within two weeks of each other. Every time I took two steps forward, it felt like I went three steps back.

Finally, after two years of treading water, of being stuck in my own way, I happened upon the whacky, wild world of personal development. It began with a book, then a seminar. Increasingly, as I gained new perspectives through the work, the inner journey began to feel like my *real* way out of the cage—and it was.

Through this inner journey, I gained clarity and strength, and expanded my vision. Within just a couple of years, it became a decision to live enthusiastically, to claim the life I truly deserved. I gave up the no-way-out point of view and began something entirely new—a journey of reverence and of service that informed, and eventually became, the With Enthusiasm™ method: a winning formula for helping overachievers like myself—like you—attain the exact same understandings and possibilities I had gained over years. I was able to change my entire life through this work. You can, too.

Helping you find satisfaction and meaning is my mission. The method you are about to experience will deliver both. It's worked for me and for the countless other overachievers I have coached—many of them just like you.

Before you start thinking, as overachievers are apt to do, "Don't worry, I can fix this on my own," stop. Though you may be full of determination and vigor, inclined to keep charging ahead, stop yourself. If you think you can fix the unease and lack of fulfillment with yet another external, temporary solution (More money? An even better job? A new, younger spouse?), the attacks from within will keep coming. Ultimately, you *will* lose. Need proof? Just look at how things are going. If things are not working out for you and you keep coming up with results that miss the mark (pure, unadulterated and lasting joy versus never feeling like anything is enough and staying in a suspended state of stress, overwhelm, and one-upmanship), try this.

Fair warning: Personal growth is seldom easy or comfortable. It does not usually look or feel great in the moment. But the end result is worth it. As Carl Jung wrote, "There is no coming to consciousness without pain." Pain is not just an inevitable part of the journey to consciousness but a necessary one. It is through the discomfort of confronting and resolving our inner conflicts and managing the real pain that life serves us that we gain insight and wisdom through which we can evolve. Pain pushes us to break free from the illusions and narratives that bind us, propelling us into a deeper understanding of our psyche and our place in the world.

The way out will not be easy and may at certain points feel to you like you stand to lose it all, but stay with it. In the end, you will find that the opposite is true: You have nothing real to lose and everything real to gain. Take a gamble on this work. Be prepared to stay the course, to complete the exercises, to reflect on the sections that take you aback (perhaps, especially those), and to achieve long-term gains.

Be willing to unlock the cage by doing the inner work. It's then that you'll be able to fly free.

CHAPTER 1

Admit It, Your Life Doesn't *Feel* as Good as It *Looks*

"I think you actually have to have all your dreams come true, to realize they're the wrong dreams."
MATTHEW PERRY

EARLY ON IN MY COACHING PRACTICE, a client confessed to me one day his reluctance to attend his Ivy League business school reunion. An old chum had told him, apparently, that "if you don't make at least $2 million a year, you shouldn't even bother coming to this thing."

First, let's face it, that's a weird thing to say to anyone, let alone someone you supposedly consider a friend. Second, objectively, my client was a superstar with enviable achievements that made him stand out well beyond any arbitrary financial milestone. He was successful, sure. But he was also funny, engaging, kind, hard-working, generous, AND in a stable, loving relationship. He had it all! So when he told me that he was considering not going to the reunion based on this comment, I was shocked. Right there, on the tip of my tongue was, "C'mon, man. *Really*?"

But I held my tongue. I was in the first year of my practice and, as green as I was, I empathized with his feelings—irrational though they seemed. I'd experienced these same feelings and these fears, as had many of my other upper-echelon clients. As overachievers, we're so susceptible to competition on all levels, to the "keeping up with the Joneses'" mentality, both in our professional and personal lives. And since you've picked up this book, chances are you empathize as well.

Overachievers often have lives that don't feel as good as they look, and they cope with this incongruity via a wide gamut of anxious thought patterns and fears. They argue for and develop reasons to justify the pace at which they are advancing socially, professionally, and financially, very rarely stopping to question whether the mountain they are climbing is even the right mountain.

Some variation of this "keep calm and carry on" attitude has likely been a part of your rise, and it has been a part of your friends' success, too. One such friend to us all was the actor Matthew Perry, who I adored as Chandler Bing. In the book he released the year before his death, *Friends, Lovers, and the Big Terrible Thing*, Perry—a bona fide superstar—detailed his struggles with drugs and admitted to standing on shaky interior ground. He had everything at his feet, including demons and addictions. In his book, Perry describes a scene similar to what my Ivy-League-reunion distraught client was experiencing. It's a hilarious, mistaken-identity story surrounding a meetup with the movie director M. Night Shyamalan—or at least a person who he thought was M. Night Shyamalan. The story involves him being gobsmacked by the "legendary director's" interest in little old him. You should read the story (and the whole book, in fact), but in the meantime, I bring up Perry and this story to say: If you are worrying about whether you measure up, whether you will ever make it to the point where you no longer feel the anxiety and pressure that comes with success, you won't. At least not through more overachieving. If the emptiness of success and the anxiety found their way to Matthew Perry's door, they can come to anyone's.

Perry exemplifies, or exemplified, what I have found to be common: There is a sadness and insecurity lying in the hearts of many ambitious people; an undercurrent of anxiety, panic, and dissatisfaction that rests beneath the carefully crafted facades. These feelings usually emerge upon the unsettling recognition that all they've attained may glisten but are not gold. Things may look shiny and safe, but in truth, they are anything but.

Truman Capote's "swans" are a testament that this truth has transcended and will continue to transcend generations. "Swans" was the moniker he gave his gaggle of gorgeous friends, like Lee Radziwill, Babe Paley, and Slim Keith—the well-heeled ladies of the Upper East Side, women of extraordinary wealth and status whom he famously betrayed in the *Esquire* article, "La Cote Basque." The moniker was a reference to the hidden effort his elegant friends took to maintain their immaculate facades—a swan gliding upon the water effortlessly but beneath the surface furiously paddling to keep up with the others. Grace on the surface but a constant struggle for their position underneath.

We are all, in a sense, attempting to be swans, desperately swimming and swimming beneath regal, but extremely bulky, feathers. Capote's subjects, like me before finding the subject of personal development—and my clients prior to coaching—found a semblance of perfection in outward appearances. We adorned ourselves with shiny trinkets that appeared to outsiders as flawless and golden, but once the luster fell off, we recognized they were never golden at all. We realized that instead of attaining what we'd been pursuing—freedom—we ended up in a glittering cage through our heedless pursuit of external success. We'd been gilded by our own ambitions.

In my coaching practice, where I deal with high-performers day in and day out, I've coined a term for this phenomenon, one I see time and time again: *The Overachievement Paradox.*[1] The paradox is of appearing to have it all and yet being discontent. Once you look like you have it all, you feel a pressure to maintain that look—defeating any semblance of peace.

Rather than episodic, The Paradox is more like stumbling on a neurosis. It's less "in the moment stress or disappointment" and more "constant state of teetering between one-upmanship and paranoia." It's a form of cognitive dissonance that convinces the wealthy they'll run out of money. It drives the brilliant to second guessing their intellect. It tells the exhausted they need to work harder to always be the best, have the best, and look the best. The Paradox also comes at a high price: perpetual self-sacrifice at the altar of achievement, which destroys the quality of your relationships—because very hard-working, obsessive, single-minded overachievers can be...*at times, a bit mean to themselves and to everyone else, too.*

This phenomenon doesn't just cost you a chance to attend your class reunion and catch up with old friends. It's a form of self-sabotage that can result in much worse: messy debt, ugly divorces, loveless marriages, intimacy issues, infidelity, isolation, paranoia, mistrust, harsh management styles, alcohol abuse, drug or doom-scrolling addictions, workaholism, strained familial and business relationships, loneliness, and physical illness. And the most common form of sabotage of them all? *Aimlessness.*

---

1   See: "The Superstar Paradox," https://www.davidpublisher.com/Public/uploads/Contribute/5db68ac761465.pdf

Aimlessness is harboring, for long stretches of time, a feeling that life is moving along but that you have not yet found your purpose—that you are somehow stuck even though you are in perpetual motion. Sure, you are living, but you aren't lit up. You are doing all the right things but missing your potential.

Do any of these strike a chord?

If so, here's what they all have in common: They've all appeared as a result of misdirecting our aim. Instead of striving for happiness, we chased surrogates like fancy titles, big houses, or money for money's sake. Those rewards end up feeling like aimlessness or loneliness because we never cared about them that much to begin with. **Ambitious people do not focus *on* happiness.** We focus on *surrogates* for happiness. *After all, why be happy when you can be rich? Or famous? Or powerful?* Given that many overachievers have spent their lives getting high marks, growing businesses, building wealth, winning awards, marrying other overachievers, and socializing with A-list celebrities, it's no wonder we have missed contentment by turning external stimuli into reality—ending up being as "real" as reality television.

Worse still, behind the veneer of success are burned-out souls suffering from narcissism, fear, anger, and depression[2] as a result of constantly banging up against this superficial reality. This can have devastating effects not only on the health and psyche of the individual but also on spouses, children, business partnerships and organizations, and subordinate employees. Though overachievers are often highly compensated, money isn't enough to offset the pressures of the corporate shark-eat-shark environment. The resulting pressure leads "externally perfect" executives caught in The Overachievement Paradox to explode in short-tempered anger and fear that stymies forward-thinking decision-making. Thus, ambitious, hard-working overachievers like yourself often experience sleepless nights and feel isolated, believing they have no one in whom to truly confide—allowing depression to settle in.

When high-profile figures, such as iconic fashion designer Kate Spade; TV celebrity Anthony Bourdain; nineties icons Stella Tenant, Chris Cornell, and Dolores O'Riordan; or actor Robin Williams, die by suicide, we watch in stunned amazement. How could those with both notoriety and fortune possibly have been so unhappy? There are many Kate Spades among overachievers right now—in our offices, at our conferences, and in our homes.

---

2   William & Mary Law School research by Jayne Barnard

Are you wondering whether your driven, high-achieving ways are missing their aim, too? Here is how to self-diagnose. Ask yourself:

- Do you believe you *don't yet* have everything you want?
- Does the success of others make you jealous, annoyed, or resentful?
- Do you have trouble sleeping?
- Do you spend many moments a day in anxiety (replaying conversations, running doomsday scenarios of possible failures, losses, and rejections)?
- Do you frequently experience sadness, negative emotions, and mood swings?
- Do you feel an unyielding pressure to not only perform but to out-perform your peers (and, if possible, the whole world)?
- Do you feel like you do many things—stay in relationships, maintain participatory status—out of obligation?

If you answered yes to any of the above, you are an overachiever and likely face similar neuroses.

In an anonymous survey conducted with more than 1,000 people earning $250,000+ and holding high degrees of education, 53 percent answered **yes** to all of the above. Even in our current economy, a surprising portion of American professionals report feeling unhappy. In the mid-1980s, roughly 61 percent of workers told pollsters they were satisfied with their jobs. Today, that number has declined substantially, hovering around half. The lowest point being in 2010, when only 43 percent of workers were satisfied, according to data collected by the Conference Board, a nonprofit research organization. The rest said they were unhappy or, at best, neutral about how they spent the bulk of their days. Even studies among professionals in medicine and law noted a rise in discontent. As for overachievers, research suggests we may be depressed at more than double the rate of the public. For example, prominent psychiatrist Michael Freedman found that nearly half (49 percent) of entrepreneurs said they experienced mental health issues at some point in their lives.

This discontent comes with an entire Pandora's box of effects, too, because overachievers are unlikely to deal with malaise or openly share it. A few examples of the most common stances I've observed in coaching sessions are:

- Exhibiting mental arrogance—the state of believing you know everything and that you've "got this"
- Having a fear of making mistakes and of perceived failure (of self and others)

- Upholding an invulnerable stance/pretense and saving face
- Displaying an impenetrable stance, a lack of vulnerability (ability to admit your own mistakes or imperfections), lack of empathy for self and others
- Being too heavily dependent upon the opinions of others
- Asserting status by people-pleasing; trying to be all things to all people
- Believing success only comes as it relates to power, money, or status
- Creating self-imposed limitations based on original/early-stage perceptions of goals/arbitrary success benchmarks

These issues can be extremely common among high-achieving individuals. They can also be debilitating and interfere with healthy functioning, effective communication, and interpersonal dynamics. All too often, addiction, depression, and anxiety may not be readily apparent to the individual suffering from these challenges or to those people working and living alongside them, which complicates things further. If *you* can relate to any of the above, **the hardest part will be admitting that you have a problem**. But if you *are* open to change and commit to doing the work, you will find happiness, satisfaction, and joy.

Case in point: My client that was going to skip his reunion? He committed to doing the internal work, the work laid out in this book. The result? He went to his reunion, showed up with no pretenses, mingled with no veneer, and reported back that he had a really good time—*free of his own gilded cage*. That may sound like a small achievement, but it was the day he opened his own cage door.

If you are up for the rest of this journey, start by admitting that what you've got going on is not working and realize what's off is that you think "you've got this" when, in fact, you do *not*.

Almost everything you have accepted as your target has been way off. It must be. After all, you are not where you think you *should* be. The admission part is up to you. There's no shame in the game. It would just be a shame if you stayed here.

PRACTICE

As we begin this journey together, sit down and:

Map out what each facet of your life would look like if you were truly happy. This can include marriage, children, extended family, friendships, professional networks, social media/networking, financial state, travel, physical fitness, self-care/beauty, fashion and style, transportation, entertainment, hobbies, and passions. If you have other areas of your life that you would like to add, do it. You'll soon see that life fulfillment means—and needs—so much more than what happens on the work front.

CHAPTER SUMMARY

1. Many people aren't as happy as they look, especially successful entrepreneurs and C-suite execs—or "overachievers."

2. The main source of dissatisfaction: the constant pursuit of success instead of happiness, which is how many, especially overachievers, measure self-worth—with a principal focus on financial status.

3. If you relate, aiming for a deeper understanding of yourself and what you want can lead to heightened success and a healthier, happier mindset. Trying to solve the malaise you feel by chasing more success (i.e., making more money) is just a bottomless pit that will never end and only begin to feel more futile.

4. This does not mean beating yourself up but merely admitting you may have less than what you truly want out of life.

5. The realization that you are not happy should not upset you or worry you (even though it might). It is the only thing that will begin to set you free because you will have changed your aim.

You Don't Know What You Don't Know

"I have not failed. I have just found 10,000 ways that won't work."
THOMAS EDISON

THE GREATEST EPIPHANY of my inner journey happened where all great epiphanies happen: SoulCycle. For those who may be unfamiliar, SoulCycle is an intense indoor spin class. It's a vibe, and occasionally, it's a place where magic happens.

I love everything about SoulCycle. I love the camaraderie of the other riders, who, like me, give off cult vibes as we pile into class wearing SoulCycle-branded attire. I love the club-like strobe lights inside the studio, the signature grapefruit-scented candle filling the air, the vibrant dance music pumping like a heartbeat, and setting up my bike feeling all "athletic"—a feat for a person who is deeply indoors-y and has never been particularly good at (or fond of) exercise. Above all, I love how the instructors toss out spiritual mantras throughout class: *"May you live your life the way you ride your bike!"*

I am happy to pay $37 for a single class, as well as carefully clear my Saturday mornings for a ride. But, on this particular day, as I was prepping my bike, something out of the ordinary happened. An older gentleman, with no prompting or invitation, reached out his hand to shake mine and said, "Hi! I'm Scott." At the time, as a New Yorker, I was taken aback at this breaking of the informal "thou shalt not talk to any stranger unless they're on fire" commandment by which New Yorkers inherently live. However, in that moment, I reminded myself that basic decency and humanity exist. I quickly decided to return the kind gesture with "Nice to meet you. I'm Keren," hoping that would end this encounter, freeing me to enjoy my spin class.

No such luck.

To my amazement, Scott did not stop talking. Not to me, not to anyone in that class. In fact, he got even louder. As the lights went down and the music turned up, he looked over at me and screamed how awesome this class was.

"I love SoulCycle! Oh my God, this is *amazing*! Wooooo-hooooooooo!" To the instructor, almost incessantly, he cried, "*Go, Caroline!*"

Here I am trying to enjoy my SoulCycle ritual, and Scott is ruining it. Fifteen minutes into class, I was outraged. I wanted to unclip, step out, and yell at the receptionist for everything that went wrong in that class. A little voice inside my head, however, reminded me that throwing a fit would be unkind. So, begrudgingly, I stayed. And so did Scott.

By the end of class, Scott had tried every single ounce of my patience. As I continued to rage internally, our instructor, Caroline, turned to us and said, "Thanks for getting through this with me, friends! I know that the guy in the front must have driven you crazy. You have to forgive him, though. That's my dad. He's just excited. I had major surgery, and we did not think I would be up here again this soon. Or ever, even. But here I am."

Wait. What now? *Scott was her dad.* He was there celebrating her life—happy she was able to continue to do what she loves. Grateful she was alive.

Seeing the full picture, I was suddenly moved to tears. Standing in that new perspective, strobe lights still overhead, I learned lesson number one, the most profound epiphany of my inner journey: Don't jump to conclusions so quickly. After all, what I had perceived about Scott—that he was a nut interrupting class for no reason—was not even the partial truth.

On my walk home, I considered this lesson. I recognized that, in life, most of the time, I wasn't seeing the full picture. Like most of us, I was certain I knew what was going on as I lived in constant evaluation of each moment. I wondered: Had I been missing the mark elsewhere due to impatience, incuriosity, and sometimes laziness?

The answer in my heart was: *Yeah, you have.*

In that moment, I learned that *when I "know" something, I kill possibilities*. It shook me. I began to detach from fixed perspectives and became slightly more willing to sit with the discomfort of not knowing.

Chances are, you believe you know what is going on most of the time. Not because you're a bad person or a rude person, but because your brain is programmed to reach for certainty in uncertain situations—so you feel in control. That's the brain's job and it works in overdrive for overachievers. To ensure the survival of our species, our brains have evolved to protect us from pain, so we feel safe. Safety requires caution; uncertainty means danger and possibly even pain. The brain is designed to conserve energy, using shortcuts to protect you from harm or pain, including uncertainty.

These shortcuts, known in the world of psychology as heuristics and cognitive bias, are attributed to researchers Amos Tversky and Daniel Kahneman, who, in 1972, proved that human judgments and decisions are not as rational as we think. Instead, Tversky and Kahneman explained that we mostly base our judgment and decision-making process on heuristics, or mental shortcuts, that ease the cognitive load of making decisions.

Examples of heuristics include using a rule of thumb, an educated guess, an intuitive judgment, or a guesstimate. As with my SoulCycle story, employing such shortcuts can backfire. Heuristics are quick, informal, and intuitive. They fail at making a correct assessment of the world. When they fail, cognitive bias occurs. This is the tendency to draw an incorrect conclusion in a certain circumstance based on familiar cognitive factors that tripped you up before. What if after SoulCycle, I classified proximity to anyone who introduced themselves as an impending threat to my class? That would not only be mean but could hinder my own experiences.

Leaning on assumptions, guesstimates, and "common sense" has been proven to hinder the ability to solve problems, come up with original ideas, and adapt to change. In other words, though your brain is well-intentioned, it is not automatically to be believed. Your brain is like my sweet, overprotective mother. It's well-meaning but will do anything it can to keep you from harm, even if it means you can never grow up and leave home. Except that to live your life fully, *you've gotta leave the house.*

Outside the SoulCycle epiphany, this greater understanding changed my life. I used to believe I knew most everything. For example, I once "knew" my career was "safe" and that I could marry "intelligently," so I did. None of which was based on actual certainty, nor worked out well. The career in my then-chosen industry of publishing radically changed. The marriage was a big mistake, flawed from its core. With time, my "safe" and "certain" choices led to a life that looked wonderful on Instagram but felt horrible and numb in real life. One day, pretty late in the game, I finally got the message: *I had to leave the safe house. I had to open my own gilded cage.*

Choosing a new perspective was how I ultimately broke through. It was when I accepted that all I could see was but a narrow sliver of what was going on—of what was possible for me—that I stopped clinging to false certainties and started reaching for real possibilities. The internal shift was enough to set me on the path that has led to right now.

To get out of any rut you must do the same: You must change your perspective. You can step into a life of far greater joy and—yes!—higher levels of success, too. For that to happen, you must accept that *certainty is ridiculous* and that anything can happen.

We are living in unprecedented times of change—the world is unfathomably complex. To believe we have mastered any level in any respect—that our angle of vision on matters like politics, philosophy, and even happiness is right all the time—is arrogant and ridiculous. This doesn't mean we ought to live in a state of perpetual doubt and uncertainty, however. If we did, we would never speak up for justice and moral truth. It does mean, though, that we're aware that what we know is, at best, incomplete.

To be clear, I am not talking about objective facts here. Facts known and scientifically validated are not subject to interpretation—only to further scientific examination. What I am talking about is **perspective on issues that rely on intersubjective beliefs and on projections**, *such as* politics, philosophy, happiness, and the future. Uncertainty is a given for all. For many people, change is terrifying, spelling doom—or worse, such as job loss, loss of control, and irrelevance. Fear and anger are understandable emotional responses, but a better and more-empowered way forward lies in rejecting the illusion of certainty in matters you have no control over.

Don't let anyone sell you certainty—not your brain, politicians, bosses, parents, or teachers. No single person or collective knows what they don't know, so buying into projections, prophecies, and promises will keep you arguing for the problem instead of focusing on the solution. Instead, **accept the momentary discomfort of uncertainty while staying curious and open**. If you do, you'll come up with solutions that will help you move forward.

Adopting humility is your greatest ally. Humility believes in collective wisdom and that we're better off surrounded with people who see the world somewhat differently than we do. Like Scott at SoulCycle: His outgoing personality and constant cheering in class was him celebrating the life of his daughter and being thrilled she is alive and well. Given the mood and perspective with which I entered that class, I am so glad Scott helped me see the world differently.

This book contains various solutions to the wide spectrum of malaise and stagnation that keeps you from the fullness of your potential and fulfillment. They require the humility of sitting with uncertainty without trying to immediately control it—challenging your perspective. *Change your perspective, change your life.*

PRACTICE: THE PAUSE PRINCIPLE

Start to counteract your reactive behavior, driven by your shortcut-loving brain, by using The Pause Principle. The Pause Principle is a mindfulness tool designed to help you slow down reactive thoughts, so you can manage uncertain situations, come to broader perspectives, and expand your possibilities.

How it works:

Every time you hit an obstacle or challenge, hit *pause*. In this moment, take these three steps:

1. **Turn inward**. Recognize your reaction is the real enemy. Getting defensive, angry, jumping to conclusions? These are the actual problems. The tipoff will be negative emotion. Stop yourself right there.

2. **Question**. Ask yourself, "Is what I see, or how I see it, the absolute truth? Is this the full story?" If it isn't, get curious.

3. **Reframe**. Ask yourself, "How can I see this as an opportunity?"

Think about a situation in your life right now. Maybe you see yourself as having worked for years in a job or a relationship with nothing to show for it. Maybe you think your business is not going well and there is a good reason to freak out.

Pause and question your situation. If in questioning the situation you observe you do not yet have the exact results you want in your life, consider that the thing standing in your way is how you have chosen to see the situation. No matter what your problems are, there is always another perspective. Your ability to control your perspective and guide it toward favorable outcomes depends on your ability to understand this and accept that you have the power to change the way you look at things.

In the words of the late spiritual teacher, Wayne Dyer, you will find that "when you change the way you look at things, the things you look at will change."

CHAPTER SUMMARY

1. You don't know what you don't know. The next time you have an impulse to jump to a conclusion, sit with it and ask yourself, "What can I learn here?"

2. The reason you even want to jump to conclusions is that the brain's default is not to keep you on the road to happiness but instead to keep you out of harm's way.

3. The more you can intercept this pattern through curiosity and inner questioning, the more you will maximize your possibilities, thus expanding your chances of not only getting positive results, but of feeling far more in charge of your life.

CHAPTER 3

The World May Be Friendlier Than You Think

"We do not see the world as it is. We see it as we are."
ANAIS NIN

IS THE WORLD FRIENDLY? Or is it hostile?

Hang on a second, don't answer immediately. This is no simple question. Your honest answer will likely point, if you truly sat down to think about this, at hostility. This, in turn, will direct you straight to the core of the "software glitch" that directs the brain into maintaining its default position (see Chapter 1). It will also point you to your dominant worldview—your philosophy or conception of the world. This is either a favorable worldview—friendly and filled with possibilities—or a worldview that is less favorable, seeing the world as having only so many resources, locked in strife and suffering. The latter view is far more common. A person who sees the world as a hostile place is generally going through this life recreating an outer world based on this inner worldview, which will result in a constant, never-ending, thankless battle. They are also considered "realistic."

It's time to consider whether "realism" is truly serving you.

We all make up stories about the reality around us based on how we perceive this reality. You have stories about where you come from, your abilities, your weaknesses, who has harmed you, and why your life is how it is right now. These stories are very convincing. You can see your bank account as low, your bed as empty, your mother-in-law as annoying, your kids as irresponsible or ungrateful, your bosses as toxic, the weather as bad, the planet as doomed, and the out-of-control government being behind it all. All of these are merely examples of your "realistic" or objective view.

I can relate. My former life consisted of many seemingly objective stories. Though they appeared very real, they were a byproduct of my worldview, and like the Soul Cycle story in Chapter 2, were far from reality. Stories like "other people are luckier than I am," "I can never become rich," and "men are [fill in the blank]" were all not objective facts, but rather born of the stance of seeing the world as an obstacle course. As a result, I had a really rough time, striving and struggling to gain or keep anything. What followed were mediocre and, sometimes, very painful results.

And they are all just stories. A bank account is neither low nor empty; it can equally be described as being open and ready to receive more. Bosses are no more toxic than your inability to see options and possibilities past the toxicity. Men can be delightfully emotionally available. These turnarounds do not point you at alternative realities, but they do point you in a new direction with greater ease and possibilities for a better reality than the one you are living right now. That's the power of challenging and changing your worldview.

If you feel like you can't solve a problem when you know that, relatively speaking, you've got it pretty good, then know it isn't all your fault. You—and many others like you—have been victims of a terrible conspiracy shaping your worldview in a negative direction. Disguised as care and protection, it ultimately aimed to convince you that the world works in Machiavellian terms: that we are competing for limited resources and that anyone having more than you means there is less available to you—that they're cheating you. This is the worldview we each inadvertently end up with, known in academic circles as a **scarcity mindset.**

A scarcity mindset has you believing there are limited resources; if someone else has something, there is less available for you. Adopting this mindset can lead you to question your worthiness, to work harder than is good for you, and to believe in—and manifest—loads of strife because, after all, nothing will be handed to you and everyone else is trying to get what you want!

Overachievers are especially susceptible to the scarcity mindset. Despite accomplishments, many may still fear failure or believe that there are not enough opportunities, resources, or recognition to go around, thus reinforcing an already negatively skewed worldview. As they rise, they compare themselves to others, constantly striving for more validation. They don't enjoy the creation of resources but instead hoard them. They resist delegating tasks instead of building careers in which they feel at ease and free. They struggle to acknowledge their own achievements, perpetuating feelings of scarcity despite outward success. It's easy to buy into this con, as it's perpetuated by pretty much everyone you know, including your parents. *Especially* your parents. And it preys upon the brain's main weakness: that it is lazy and defensive. But you bought it and that is precisely why you feel discomfort right now. You learned to see the world as hostile, and you have created suffering. This ends now. There is an alternative for you: the **abundance mindset**.

Author Stephen R. Covey coined the term "abundance mindset" in his best-selling book *The 7 Habits of Highly Effective People*. According to Covey, to have an abundance mindset is to believe that the world is full of enough replenishing resources and there is more than enough for everyone. "Abundance" explains how Taylor Swift and the internet appeared in my lifetime. It explains how our economy continues to expand even though, as my favorite teacher Esther Hicks likes to point out, "No one is trucking in new resources from other planets."

If you can reach the place of considering abundance as a theoretical possibility, your mind will be open to considering a new way to tell your life story. You will then be open to more possibilities, rather than attached to the scenarios in which life is nothing but more strife. It's more practical than "telling it like it is." After all, if you continue to argue for your present condition, you will get to keep it.

PRACTICE: THE ABUNDANCE MINDSET

First, let's find out what place you are operating from: scarcity or abundance.

1. Write down what you want. The top three crowd-pleasers in coaching are health, finances, and love, but you can choose anything you'd like.

2. Write down the specific reasons you think you *can't* have it. For example, if you answered "way more money," you might write:
    *   *It's really hard to make the kind of money I want to make.*
    *   *There are obstacles such as education, opportunities, and time.*
    *   *I have a history of not making very much money.*

3. Examine your reasons. Do they sound like abundance (possibilities still lie ahead) or scarcity (there a fixed outcome)?
    If you are operating from abundance, congratulations! Keep doing what you are doing.
    If you are operating from scarcity, go to the next step.

4. Name three reasons you *can* have what you want. For example, in keeping with the theme of bringing in more money, you could write:
   - *Someone out there has made the kind of money I want, so it is possible.*
   - *Even if it takes time and requires closing a skill gap, I have time and can do it.*
   - *Others had a history of not making very much money, including Bryan Cranston and Coach Keren; they turned it around, so I can, too.*

You can choose the abundance mindset to become your new worldview. This worldview lies at the center of modern psychology, also known as positive psychology, the study of wellbeing and mindset factors that contribute to creating a life that feels good. Its founder, Dr. Martin Seligman, spent decades researching optimism and has found that this disposition, founded purely upon the capacity to adopt an abundance mindset, is not a fixed trait. Instead, it can be seen as a strategy—an outlook that we can cultivate by challenging our automatic negative thoughts through the lens of abundance. It delivers. As Seligman says, "Life inflicts the same setbacks and tragedies on the optimist as on the pessimist, but the optimist weathers them better."

This practice is extraordinarily valuable. Dr. Seligman and countless other psychologists and researchers have proven that a more joyful outlook on life, coupled with an adopted disposition that is rationally optimistic (pragmatic, forward-thinking, and eager) are beneficial to your health, to aging, to resilience, to quality of life, to success, to relationships, and more. In other words, no matter what problem you are facing, the solution lies in getting happier or more proactive about it.

That's all you want anyway. Happiness, peace. These are synonyms, and they are the only true aim of any of our endeavors. Think about it: Anything you want, you want because you think it will make you happier. The next million? You think it will make you feel better than now, sans million. The car? You think it's a straight shot at joy. The devoted partner? So many believe that's the magic elixir. In fact, you don't need any of these. You just need to focus on abundance instead of on scarcity. On what you have and can yet gain with all the time and skills you have instead of on what you don't have and remains missing.

The choice between scarcity and abundance lies within you. If you find yourself entrenched in a scarcity mindset, it's a signal to dive deeper. There are two ways to take that dive. The first is to realize that though scarcity may be convincing (after all, you can hear, see, smell, taste, touch, and quantify what "is," making it hard for your rational brain to argue and easy for circumstances to be accepted as the total reality), it is futile. Arguing for your limitations only means you get to keep them. The point of the abundance mindset and of positive thinking is not to discredit reality but to suggest there may be other possibilities to help you overcome this perceived giant obstacle.

The second way to a more abundance-focused worldview is to deepen your inner inquiry by asking yourself, "What do I believe about the world?" In a challenging moment, a moment of anger, worry, or fear, the inquiry will keep bringing you back to who you truly are because none of us enjoys being a person who sees the world as hostile and against us. Little by little, you will employ the pause, considering that the totality of possibilities may allow you to transcend the current obstacle, and guide yourself back to abundance. And, ultimately, to happiness.

CHAPTER SUMMARY

1. Our worldview is how we see the world or our core philosophy about our reality. It answers the questions: What is the nature of the world? Is it ordered, fair, and abundant? Or is it competitive, ruthless, and chaotic? Whichever stance you hold will impact your beliefs (Chapter 2) and ultimately guide your reactions (Chapter 1). Therefore, it is best to question and examine your worldview.

2. The best place to find out which worldview you subscribe to is to examine the stories you tell about your circumstances (or your "reality"). Your worldview is perpetuated and revealed by the stories you tell yourself. You have stories about where you come from, what abilities you have, what weaknesses you have, who has harmed you, and why you are where you are in your life right now. These are by-products of seeing the world as a big, bad obstacle course, which then leads you to adopting what is known as a scarcity mindset.

3. A scarcity mindset is a set of attitudes and beliefs that are founded upon the notion that there are limited resources in the world, and we are all competing for the same finite, or scarce, pool. It causes hyperfixation, leads to short-term coping instead of long-term problem-solving, and increases jealousy and stress. Even worse, it is ultimately keeping you from your true potential.

4. In contrast, an abundance mindset is when you believe that the world is full of enough resources and time for you to accomplish your goals, that resources are ever-replenishing on this planet, and thus, there is more than enough for everyone.

5. When given the option between scarcity and abundance, always choose abundance. The main difference is that, with a scarcity mindset, everything gets smaller, rarer, and less possible. But with an abundance mindset, everything gets exponentially bigger, becomes easier, and is more available. It is the road to the totality of possibilities, and it can be learned and cultivated.

CHAPTER 4

Don't Always Believe
What You Think

"What we resist, persists."
CARL JUNG

WHILE TEACHING THE PAUSE PRINCIPLE at one of my earliest coaching retreats, I invited the audience to participate in the reframing exercise. One man angrily raised his hand and shouted, "My wife cheated on me, left me, and is now married to the other *schmuck*. Are you telling me that's *not the real problem*?"

"No, that's not what I said," I replied, clarifying that I wasn't saying cheating didn't happen, nor denying it was a difficult thing for him to go through. It *did, and it is.*

I was simply asking him to consider that the cheating did not happen *to* him but rather that the idea of slight was the real problem—asking him to question his perspective of being cast as the victim. I invited him to ponder that the cheating had possibly happened *for* him. Or that it just **happened.**

Once he opened to inquiry, I asked him a few questions to see if we could expand his view and our possibilities. I asked him if he and his wife had been growing apart before the rupture occurred. He shuffled for a bit and then admitted that they had been for years, adding they were rarely intimate. Next, I asked about their careers. He said that while her career thrived, his career had taken a nosedive in the last years of their marriage, and he may not have been very gracious about this discrepancy. We were able to conclude that this problem had not appeared completely out of the blue. Things seldom do.

With more time and gentle questioning, this man was able to reframe his belief from "the cheating happened *to* me" to "the cheating happened." And while we did not get all the way to "the cheating happened *for* me" that day, that reframe eventually came over the following months. Seeing his wife's departure as just something that happened, no longer as charged with ego-defeating meanings, he was able to move on and regain his strength.

A few years have passed since, and I am happy to report that this man is now successfully remarried and happily co-parents with his ex-wife and her new husband. So what happened? What was blocking him from getting to this point faster? What took this man so long to get past a slight and to the next level of his life? It turns out that it was not merely his perspective—it was his limiting beliefs.

A limiting belief is a thought held for a long time, one that is believed to be the absolute truth, thus limiting options and stopping you from doing certain things. Limiting beliefs can be about yourself, about the world, about ideas, and/or about other people and their behaviors, intentions, and actions. They are all founded upon the scarcity worldview, and they keep you anchored into your position, making the possibility of emerging into a new and improved reality much harder than it could be.

This man's beliefs about what happened were doing just that: They had boxed him into a corner. In his mind, cheating was a cardinal offense, in which he was a victim, he had been wronged, and there were no two ways about it. He even shared that, in his house, the name of the lover could never be mentioned. Not even after the two got married. These types of thoughts, or limiting beliefs, became the distance between where he was and where he wanted to be: free.

I see this over and over again when coaching overachievers. Successful strivers set a high standard (condition) for themselves that can, at first, help them achieve remarkable things, but it can also set the stage for limiting beliefs that can ultimately block their potential and their happiness. Many start believing, for example, that they have to constantly outdo themselves to be considered successful or worthy. They *must*. It's like they're stuck in this never-ending race against their own expectations. This, then, becomes not a belief that empowers them but one that cements their feet to the ground.

This tendency can veer into the cruelest and most rigid of pursuits, the pursuit not only of high standards but of perfection. If you are wondering what the difference between these two is, it's that high standards don't necessarily hurt.

Perfectionist standards, built entirely upon limiting beliefs such as "I must work out every day," "I must be successful," "I must be very rich," and "I must never gain weight", *do*. A perfection seeker will turn on himself each and every time the arbitrary hallmark ("rich," "thin," "successful," "relevant/ important") will be missed, making the distance between him and where he wants to be—free—even vaster.

If you feel stuck, trapped behind an invisible wall blocking your full potential, it's likely a pile of limiting beliefs that is causing your frustration, rather than actual circumstances. Here's the great news: If you would like to close that gap, all you need to do is learn how to identify your limiting beliefs and learn how to loosen them up so they no longer stand in your way.

The reason it's important to manage these limiting beliefs is because they are limiting you (literally, they are keeping you from the joy and fulfillment and success you deserve) because they are not truths. Most of them are just assumptions/ shortcuts your brain has made for you. Sure, some of them got you to where you are today, but here's the deal: Most of them will not get you *there*—to where you want to go, to true freedom. You will find they actually form an invisible barrier between the two. With them, you can go far but not as far as if you dump them.

I vote to dump them.

Specifically, let's dump the limiting ones. If you are cool with ideas like money is finite and time is *really* finite, fine, keep them. But if you are not, then accept that they are limiting beliefs and that they are not 100% true—that they limit your happiness and possibilities. A limiting belief is not only false, it is also pointed in the wrong direction. It's a thought pattern focused on problems and obstacles that seeks to separate and judge instead of to align and ignite. You will find that it reinforces itself. Those of us who do not check these will keep stumbling into circumstances that just confirm the problems and the obstacles— not get past them. For example, the workshop participant. He believed that his wife's cheating was the real problem, causing him to continue in a holding pattern, stuck in unhappiness and blame, when it was actually the stuckness in this disgruntled belief that was the problem. Continuing to cling to it would maintain his stance and his stunted state, too.

In contrast, a positive (unlimited) belief is a thought pattern focused on solutions. This kind of belief can get you through present circumstances, straight to innovative solutions, and even breakthroughs that defy great odds. For example, in 2019, my mom was diagnosed with stage 4 melanoma (skin cancer). By the time this was discovered, it had spread everywhere—her lungs, colon, liver. The doctors gave her a pretty low chance of surviving, even with the recommended treatment course of immunotherapy.

At first, my mom—a giant buzzkill by nature (her mantra is literally "hope for the best, prepare for the worst")—looked at the prognosis as a probable impending doom. From the moment the doctor shared it, she inadvertently began preparing for the worst and focusing on her limiting beliefs. That is until I offered a different perspective: my fervent belief in the power of changing limited beliefs to *unlimited* beliefs. I encouraged her to see the real possibility that she *could* survive. She ended up doing just that; she chose to believe in possibility and is today, four years later, free and clear of any cancer.

This is the power of believing better.

We all experience our own limiting beliefs, and they are as common as they are NBD (*no big deal*). Many of them were bestowed early in life by teachers, religion, physical conditions, and family members, all mostly well-meaning. Oftentimes, these beliefs are imparted innocently, as ways to protect us from pain and suffering but often end up making us feel even worse. For example, a deeply held belief conveyed in the old cliche that "money doesn't grow on trees'" is intended to spare us a life of frivolity and lack but can open us up to financial shame and guilt with any purchase we make, leading directly *to* frivolity and lack. As these beliefs amass, our perspective grows narrower, fixated on an ever-shrinking set of options—and our sense of fear and despair grows.

The more ingrained beliefs become, the more they inform our stories, the ways in which we explain ourselves, justify our attitudes, and make our choices, which gradually start to backfire, as these slow us down and eat us up inside. If you are struck with a recurring problem and revisiting it so often you feel as if you are in purgatory, chances are, there's a limited belief there. A belief, or even belief system, is narrowing your perspective and, therefore, limiting your possibilities. Even those that seem innocuous. For example:

- *There are no good men/women.*
- *I have "a thousand" emails.*
- *I don't have enough money.*
- *I can never get ahead.*
- *I'm running out of time.*

Most of these sound reasonable to those who do not question their beliefs. They are not. They keep us stunted, insecure, and paranoid. Luckily, there is a quick way to take all the air out of them, exposing them for what they are: phony baloney. The way to unpack them is to tell the story differently. Think about it:

- Are there *no* suitable candidates for dating? Really? Not even one?
- Aren't half those emails just spam and CCs? And couldn't you get through them in under an hour?
- Haven't you made money in the past? If so, isn't it possible you could earn more and acquire what you really want at some point?
- Isn't there some example out there of a human who, at your age, still set out to do and did what they truly wanted to do?
- Have you heard of anyone overcoming your illness? I'll bet they are out there. Which means you might overcome this, too.

Whenever you come up against beliefs that are not useful, you can engage in a mental exercise of questioning them until the suffering is gone. To this end, there is a four-question sequence known simply as The Work created by spiritual teacher Byron Katie. It is by far the best way I have found to identify and question the persistent thoughts (beliefs) that cause suffering and come between you and your dreams. It is a way to find peace with yourself and with the world.

Here's how to do it: Simply meet a negative belief, such as, "I don't have enough [fill in the blank]" with four simple questions:

Is that true?

Is that 100% true?

Who are you being when you believe this thought?

Who would you be without the thought?

The Pause Principle can serve you here, too, but The Work takes you a longer distance by not only reframing your perspective but also challenging you to see that, in agreeing to a limited perspective, *you* are holding yourself back—and keeping yourself and your life possibilities small.

Important note: Not all limiting beliefs are bad. Most limiting beliefs mean: "This is what I do not want" or "This is the opposite of my desire." There is immense benefit to discovering these, for as you turn them around, you turn yourself around and can move more swiftly in the direction of your desire. It is painful for you to stay separate from your desire. If you decide to stay in such a negative pattern, you will get more of what you do not want, more separateness from desire. If you are willing to do The Work and to challenge your beliefs, you will overcome them and soar to the fullness of your potential.

PRACTICE: DO THE WORK

Your thoughts and beliefs create your reality as they determine your possibilities, so let's hone in on the ones that do not serve you. Write down any notion that feels uncomfortable, those that typically begin with I can't, I always, I never, I am not good at, I don't deserve, I can't afford, I'm not good enough for, I'm not worthy of, I wish I could, or *someday, I will*...

Here are some examples from real-life clients:

- *I can't afford the lifestyle I really want.*
- *I can't lose weight.*
- *Relationships are hard work and end poorly.*
- *I can't have a career that is balanced, fulfills me,* and *pays well. It's either/or.*
- *Dating is hard.*
- *I am alone and can trust only myself.*
- *Other people are ahead of me.*
- *I can't get ahead.*
- *I have messed up.*
- *Money comes to those who already have it.*
- *The world is getting worse; the next generation is screwed.*

Identify some of your own beliefs. Write them out.

_____

_____

_____

_____

_____

_____

_____

Next, examine each belief. Ask yourself:

Are these beliefs _true_?

Are they 100% true?

Who are you being when you believe this?

Who would you be without this belief?

_____

_____

_____

_____

_____

_____

_____

The key to your transformation into a happier person is to realize that your beliefs are just thoughts that you've had for a long time, that they are not serving you, and that you _can_ change them. As you continue to practice, you will realize that the true freedom lies in recognizing that you are not bound by the confines of old beliefs but rather liberated by the infinite possibilities of new ones.

CHAPTER SUMMARY

1. We all have our beliefs, many of which are bestowed upon us rather early in life by teachers, religion, physical conditions, and family members. They shape our belief systems and worldview, but we *can* change them.

2. That is the good news. We can manage our beliefs.

3. Next time you uncover a belief, ask yourself if your beliefs are true, then go through inner questioning. You will often find the beliefs have not been serving you. You can challenge and change them.

4. Changing your limiting beliefs takes work and repetition, but it's worth it.

CHAPTER 5

You're *Not* Playing to Win

*"I've heard Warren [Buffet] say a half dozen times,
'It's not greed that drives the world, but envy.'"*
CHARLIE MUNGER

EVER HEARD THE STORY OF LUPE VELEZ?

Urban legend and the turn of the century TV series *Frasier* (my favorite sitcom of all time) have it that Lupe Velez was a vain movie star in the 1930s who struggled to become famous. Above all things, Velez, who was beautiful, young, and had everything going for her, wanted to be remembered forever. So, after years of trying to get her movie career off the ground and seeing that her career was not taking off, she planned to become immortal through extreme means: by staging a lavish suicide. She would overdose and lie in her beautiful negligee on her satin sheets to die. Alas, for her last meal, she chose Mexican food and it did not sit well with the pills she took to end her life. As she ran into the bathroom, she tripped and fell head-first into the toilet. Which was how they found her.

I'm pretty sure you will remember her and that story forever.

The message in the fable is clear: Be careful what you wish for because you just might get it.

Many of us don't consider what we are asking for when we ask for success, fortune, and fame. We may be asking for a completely undesirable outcome. As we cycle through a never-ending chase behind illustrious friends for any chance to win or outrank them, we end up just like Lupe—in the dumps.

The question is: *Are we overachievers primed for thinking in a way that ends up with us getting results we don't even like?*

It is a fascinating question with a fascinating answer (in a nutshell: yes) and well worth your while to understand psychologically. In this chapter, I want to briefly discuss why or how you got to this place or why anyone gets to a place in which they appear to have gotten what they want but don't really want it.

It's summarized neatly in the 2018 mega-hit romantic comedy *Crazy Rich Asians*. In the opening scene, the protagonist, Rachel Chu (played by Constance Wu), a professor at NYU, is teaching an economics class a valuable lesson through a poker match with her teaching associate, whom she easily defeats in spite of his having a very good hand while she had nothing. After Chu's glorious victory, she explains that the reason she won, even though her hand was empty, was that she knew her teaching associate would not play with his logic but rather with his psychology. His psychology dictated that he would be driven primarily by loss aversion—the fear of losing. It is then that she utters the sentence that frames the entire movie: "Our brains so hate the idea of losing something that's valuable to us that we abandon all rational thought, and we make some really poor decisions. So, Curtis wasn't playing to win. **He was playing not to lose.**"

This, friends, is the great irony in overachievers: Thinking you are playing to win when you are only playing to dominate. Like Lupe Velez, you may, in spite of good and earnest intentions, lay yourself a trap.

A well-known economics study published in 1995 illustrates our flawed psychology exquisitely. Participants were asked their income preferences, in relation to others:

- Option A: Your current yearly income is $50,000; others earn $25,000.
- Option B: Your current yearly income is $100,000; others earn $200,000.

Get this. They found that 56 percent of participants chose **Option A**, suggesting that these participants were willing to give up a substantial amount of absolute income in favor of gaining a relative "upper hand." People were willing to make half as much money if they made more than those around them—and they viewed success in terms of comparing themselves to others. Sounds bananas, right? Yet that's how most overachievers play. In a study published by the National Bureau of Economic Research, this phenomenon has been called "Last Place Aversion,"[3] when you worry

---

3   https://www.npr.org/2011/09/04/140116142/avoiding-last-place-some-things-we-dont-outgrow

not about the absolute bottom line but about not out-doing someone else in your Young Presidents' Organization (YPO) forum. Not ending up…last.

In one of his talks, investor Warren Buffet said he is familiar with this phenomenon and finds it baffling: "You can give someone a $2 million bonus and they're happy until they see the next guy got $2.1 million and then they're miserable." Comparing yourself to others can lead to dissatisfaction, even if you are financially successful. But here's what it can also lead to: becoming a mediocre player. The player for whom enough is never enough is the player who ultimately never wins.

Like it or not, the problem is that there will always be someone getting richer faster than you. Stating the obvious, playing for top billing is not a great way to live your life because it is never going to work out. (Sorry, Elon.) Understanding this also holds one of the keys to breaking free—that getting stuff (achievements, money, partner, acclaim) misses the point. It may make you even less happy than you were before. Chasing scarcity only ends with more scarcity.

Checking your intention and aiming higher emotionally (for abundance) will set you on the right track. For the disciplined few, with lots of practice, this is a straight shot. For most, life will happen, things will invariably come up, and you will have to keep checking yourself. You will need to find a way to completely reframe competition as a motivator.

It's hard for some people to stop caring about being the best and having the most money to show for it. Having faith in your own value—without your accomplishments—is petrifying. If you have been going through a problem for a very long time, you will take a bit longer to join me here, and it makes sense. You think the solution resides in whatever will accomplish the target—get the deal done, sell the company, land the job, land the partner. But keep calm and read on.

Abundance is a concept that many embrace because it seems terrific. It's the idea of a *win-win*; nothing but possibility. But it doesn't take root while loss aversion, or last-place aversion (zero-sum thinking), is still your driving emotion.

This next segment is an operating manual to allow yourself to expand further into abundance and out of antiquated, self-defeating modes of operation. Take some time with it. You never read operating manuals all at once, right? So take your time here. Slow down, redirect, and pivot those distressing thoughts that are too fixated on "getting this sorted." Give yourself a moment to see the bigger, far better picture.

Aiming to understand our psychology better will allow us to do just that. According to cognitive behavioral theory, several important thinkers, and self-help "guru" Tony Robbins, humans operate from six basic emotional needs. No, not your physical survival needs like shelter, water, or food (aka Maslow's hierarchy of needs) but instead your basic emotional needs. The way you prioritize these will wire your thinking and behavior.

THE SIX EMOTIONAL NEEDS

- The most basic emotional need is **certainty**. This need has a broad range—everything from wanting comfort in your environment at work and at home or that relationships you value stay secure.
- Next is **significance**. This is the need to know that you matter, that you are loved, that you are needed. This isn't about approval or validation; rather, this is the need to hold importance in another's life.
- Just as you need certainty, you also need **uncertainty**. Uncertainty can signal variety but is also about needing problems or challenges, too. It's through tough situations that you develop emotional range.
- The fourth need is that of **love and connection**. This is the holy grail—the very reason you are here on this earth. You are here to love and to connect with other humans.
- Next is the need for **progress and growth**. It's why you strive in life. Every person's happiness depends on growth—from spiritual growth to the growth you experience having new adventures and learning new things.
- The sixth and final human need is to **contribute beyond yourself,** which is essentially the need to share. We're talking about a Gandhi-level share, which means altruistic sharing and doing so with no need or desire for credit or reward. Most people, bogged down by fear, won't get to see this in their lifetime.

If your life feels like it has gone off track or is stuck in some rut, if it feels incomplete even if you are making traction toward your desired solution, if it keeps being met with situations that you find difficult, or if you have everything you've ever wanted but still lie awake at night waiting for the other shoe to drop while aimlessly scrolling TikTok, it is likely that you have been (and continue to be) overprioritizing the first two needs: **certainty** and **significance**. This is likely to be what has fueled, aid-ed, and abetted the creation of limiting and perfectionist beliefs. Overemphasizing these, or playing for these "lower" needs, is playing defense (playing "not to lose"). This ends up blocking or obstructing the four needs that reside above them.

Want to take some risks and expand into greater possibilities? If so, know that a continued adherence to certainty and fear of any change will make you allergic to any of it, even great new adventures like marriage, skiing, or a new cuisine.

Seeking real love?
- Not if you associate it with the terror of losing love (certainty) or with losing face after divorce (significance). In this case, if you are certainty- and significance-driven, you will end up with a roommate or, at best, a good-looking business partner but not a lover.

Want to launch a business, scale a business, grow emotionally, or just grow?
- You are reaching for the fifth emotional need but watch out! If certainty and significance are at the helm, you will be too afraid of the risk, rejection, failure, criticism, and even glory on the other side of growth. The result? Snoozefest instead of *Forbes* list.

Want to make an impact on the world that is positive and to truly contribute beyond yourself to the community and our planet?
- You can kiss that idea goodbye if you are still obsessed with doing it "safely" or with getting recognized for it.

Certainty and significance are useful only to a moderate extent. When they inform and inspire the majority of your actions, they keep you in neutral, even when it outwardly looks like you are "climbing."

To break on through to the other side, you will have to cut loose from your attachment to these— to certainty, your comfort zone, your need to know, your need to be right, to your significance, to your need for validation. When you do, you will stop playing **not to lose and start playing to win.**

How do you play to win? By identifying your emotional state and aiming higher.

The way to play to win is to become adept at identifying emotions associated with either certainty, significance, or higher emotional needs. There are emotions that create and emotions that stop or destroy. Knowing the difference, and beginning to choose how to act, will activate new patterns and new outcomes.

Below is a chart of these emotions. Once you identify them, as you create anything, you will know whether you are driving from fear (scarcity) or from love (abundance). This can help you self-correct, as only abundance will create the highest and most lasting results.

HIGHER EMOTIONS love and growth	LOWER EMOTIONS certainty and significance
1. calm	1. fear
2. hope	2. shame
3. peace	3. blame
4. eagerness	4. resentment
5. enthusiasm	5. regret
6. joy	6. defiance
7. excitement	7. frustration
8. gratitude/appreciation	8. anger
9. acceptance	9. defensiveness

PRACTICE

Are you going after anything new or big right now? A job interview, a business pitch, an exciting dating prospect? If so, observe your thoughts and actions around this situation.

IDENTIFY YOUR EMOTIONS.

How do you feel right now?
Write down the feelings.

Are your emotions, as you approach this new thing, in the lower or higher categories above?
Write this out.

If they are lower, what action can you take or which mindset tool can you employ to turn upwards?
Write this out.

POSTSCRIPT
SELF-SABOTAGE: WHEN WE PLAY NOT TO LOSE—AND LOSE ANYWAY

While writing this book, I watched an awesome documentary, *The Donut King*, about Ted Ngoy, a Cambodian refugee who built a multimillion-dollar empire baking America's favorite pastry. The story is heartwarming and heartbreaking all at once. It follows Ngoy's arrival in California in the 1970s after escaping the brutal Khmer Rouge in Cambodia. He eventually started his first donut shop in Orange County, California, rapidly expanding into a chain of success. Over the next decade, Ngoy also sponsored hundreds of visas for incoming Cambodian refugees and offered them steady employment in his donut shops. So far: heartwarming.

But after living his version of the American dream, everything came crashing down. He developed an addiction to gambling, a terrible, all-consuming addiction that led to the destruction of his fortune, his marriage, and, to an extent, his reputation. Watching the documentary, it was apparent that Ngoy, for all his gifts, did not ever bet on, nor accept, his own success.

This is common for people who achieve and reach great heights, especially if they were raised in a lacking or traumatic environment. Whatever is learned in childhood about worth can easily and readily smack you into submission during adulthood. You will not only hedge against real wins, you will sabotage any that come your way.

Have you ever noticed that, right after you secure the dream job, find a great relationship, or finally feel genuinely happy with everything you need, that's exactly when you feel overcome with stress, worry, doubt, and fear?

It's not a coincidence—it's self-sabotage.

It's the brain's subconscious way of ensuring you stay within your "safe zone." If you are not accustomed to feeling good for long stretches of time, your mind registers that as foreign and, potentially, dangerous. When you have everything you want, you are more vulnerable than ever before because you could lose it all. Instead of enjoying it, you may find yourself becoming paranoid and neurotic because there's a lot on the line.

Gay Hendricks, the author of *The Big Leap,* calls this the upper limit. The upper limit, he explains, is a cap for how much happiness you will allow yourself. It backs up the idea that what you are seeking in life is not happiness but comfort as you continue to work to satisfy your needs of certainty and significance, rather than any of your higher emotional needs. In turn, this can result in overt self-sabotage, beginning with selling yourself short or toning yourself down. It results in a life where you don't step fully into your genius but rather hold back on the full potential of what you have to offer. It results in shining brightly but not enjoying the fruits of your success, either experiencing the arrival of success with numbness, guilt, or dissatisfaction. Inevitably, you will turn on yourself. And that's when playing not to lose will spiral straight in the direction of total loss.

CHAPTER SUMMARY

1. Most overachievers think they are playing to win. They are not. In fact, they are "playing not to lose." Loss aversion is so fixed in our minds, we would rather forgo the possibilities of endless joy to maintain some semblance of meager comfort.

2. Loss aversion is informed by the same worldview and limiting beliefs discussed in prior chapters but is kept in place by lower-level emotional needs, managing to sow even more chaos: the chaos of limiting your potential.

3. There are six basic emotional needs, the "bottom" two of which—certainty and significance—are perhaps adept at keeping you safe but are also keeping you from being happy.

4. If you feel concerned, confused, unfulfilled, unhappy with your life results and prospects ahead and overwhelmed or paralyzed at the thought of true growth, it is likely that certainty and significance have been at the helm of your emotional needs.

5. Once you identify that your emotional default is set to certainty and/or significance, examine your thoughts. Aim to focus more on certainty and growth rather than on hedging your bets and playing it safe.

6.   To play to win is to become adept at identifying emotions associated with certainty and significance and learning how to overwrite (manage) them. There are emotions that create and those that stop or destroy. Knowing the difference will activate new patterns and new outcomes. It will also point you to the higher emotions, all associated with happiness, ensuring that the ultimate target remains your primary focus.

CHAPTER 6

Detox Your Mindset

"Happiness is a direction, not a place."
SYDNEY J. HARRIS

THERE COMES A MOMENT in your life where you stop and wonder, "What the heck is going on around here?" If you experience it, this is a moment that may bring you to a higher ground.

For me, that miracle moment was when my home was burgled. I know, sounds like a highly unlikely path to enlightenment but hear me out. Thieves broke into my building and stole my handbag, which, on that day, contained all my jewelry, my laptop, and my passport, too. This was devastating and was about to get worse. I immediately learned, while filing the report with the police, that my husband had not paid our insurance bills, so none of the stolen items were insured or covered. It was a total loss.

Speaking of total loss, my marriage was a total loss by that point, too. At the time of said burglary, my husband and I were already alienated from each other. Barely able to stand the sight of him, I slept on the other side of our apartment. At least there I could sleep with my cats since my then-husband hated animals and did not allow them in the bedroom.

I was in a haze. Nothing felt right. I was going through the motions. The day of the burglary, having lost so many important things, in the shower I finally let myself feel the pain. Sobbing while listening to Abba's "My Love, My Life," I thought, "What am I even *doing* with my life?"

Crying so hard, thinking I would never get out of this, I turned ABBA off, stepped out of that shower, dried my eyes, and made a decision. It wasn't the decision to get divorced, to quit my job, to leave Switzerland, to go back home to New York City. (Don't worry, the story ends well, and I did all those things.)

The decision was to accept some responsibility and to figure out how I, a person who had done everything "right," had ended up here, with no passion for my own life. I made this decision with no self-pity. Anyone can lose their passion for life. Anyone can go off course, and I already knew this. Yes, that means your life can go off course, too. Many of us don't like to accept or admit this, but we do know it. We have all invariably lived through times when we rocked life, when we were the leaders of our packs, when we worked in jobs that meant something to us, when we looked forward to each day, when we believed in our dreams, and when we laughed a lot. Then, inevitably, things just did not continue to work out the way we wanted. That job grew stale, someone did us wrong, our marriage turned out to be imperfect or dissatisfying, our weight and health fluctuated, and we noticed that our crowd was maybe not so high vibe. Or, sometimes, we were just tired and burnt out. Things took much longer than we thought. *C'est la vie.*

Isn't it good to know that no matter where you've been or where you are now, you can still enter into a new era—a vastly different one—simply by pointing in a new direction? In the total-loss moment, that was what I was about to find out. I was about to discover that there was a next stage.

This is what author David Brooks, a conservative political and cultural commentator who writes for *The New York Times,* called "The Second Mountain" in his book of the same name. Its central argument is about having a moment of reckoning—a fork in the road. This moment arrives for many of us who have been following culture's scripts and prescriptions. It has us confront the fact that so many of the things we have been pursuing in adulthood are more trouble than they're worth.

It's bad enough that you've failed to achieve your career ambitions, win the respect of your peers, or fashion a comfortable lifestyle. In some ways, it's worse if you are a successful overachiever because then it's all too obvious that such things don't bring deep fulfillment. In Brooks' book's governing metaphor, you've made it to the summit of life's first mountain, only to discover that the view isn't so great and you feel empty inside. The truly joyful people are those, often impelled by a shock such as divorce or bereavement, who find their second mountain, abandoning themselves to a greater cause, forgoing the life they'd wanted. This is when you might head onto the second mountain: the mountain of joy, purpose, and expansion that lies ahead.

Now that I am here, after the burglary, the rupture, and the rebuild, I know what this mountain feels and looks like—happy. A great definition of happiness is provided by the inspirational speaker known as Abraham Hicks: the state of being *"satisfied with what is and eager for more."* If you're looking for a more scientific definition, Dr. Martin Seligman, the "father" of positive psychology, developed a model of happiness that includes five core elements of a life of fulfillment, happiness, and meaning that includes positive emotion, a feeling of engagement in life and in your life's work, good relationships, and a sense of meaning. I've got all of these. It is great up here. You are going to love the view.

It will take deliberate and sustained effort to course correct and to question the way you see the world in order to get here, but you have already begun the journey, and your process can be expedited at this juncture not only with your understanding of abundance (versus scarcity and playing "not to lose") but with a full **mindset detox**—a protocol I created—thanks to encouragement from two very unlikely people: Jane Fonda and Joel Osteen.

I'll start with Fonda. Back in the 90s, I was a chubby kid. Frankly, I blame the 80s for it, with its steady diet of Honey Nut Cheerios, Pop-Tarts, and lots of great cable TV. These perfectly matched my indoors-y and rather gluttonous tendencies. In the 80s, I knew I was chubbier than most kids, but it didn't bother me much, nor did it hinder my popularity. Having been blessed with a preternaturally jovial and accommodating personality, I always managed to find friends to write plays with me, watch TV with me, and pass notes to me. I thought we were all fine, just as we were.

This era of innocence ended in the 90s when, at the age of 13, some kid in physical education class called me "Thunder Thighs" and the moniker stuck. Soon it was, "Hey, Thunder Thighs!" and "Thunder Thighs, can you help me with my homework?" The nickname defined me in middle school and not in a good way. That's where Jane Fonda comes in. I got a hold of *Jane Fonda's Lean Routine* on VHS. That tape was filled with gems—I mean, the best moves ever—including, if my memory serves, "the monkey" and "windshield wipers" routines.

In a mad rush to end the teasing, I worked out with Jane every day, copying her moves *and* her leotards. She made exercise fun, and she taught me more than just how to "do the pony." (Look it up. It's hilarious.) At the end of the workout, Jane spoke about the importance of eating a balanced, nutrient-rich diet and nourishing my body alongside regular exercise. It was the first time in my life that I had heard such information. My parents thought Honey Nut Cheerios with full-fat milk constituted a healthy meal. Not only was Jane my first aerobics instructor, but she was also my first nutritionist. You could say she was my first coach—and thanks to her glamorous workout outfits and obvious results (do you remember what she looked like? At 50?!) I intently listened to her advice.

What I learned from Jane Fonda has become, 30 years later, common knowledge: There are foods that cause inflammation and weight gain, the chemicals and processing in food are not necessarily a good thing, and these toxins and empty calories can build up in our systems, clog them up, and make us, well, chubby. Today, we hear similar things about sugar, fat, meat, dairy, caffeine, and gluten. Diet culture is so pervasive that most of us are familiar with the concept of a detox—a cleanse of the body to achieve optimal health through a rigorous diet that includes avoiding harmful substances.

Until Jane came along, I'd never heard the term *detox*. In 1992, the idea of eating "clean" or eating "soundly" was earth-shattering; at least it was to me. On her tape, Jane Fonda recommended I eat a certain diet, stay away from harmful stuff, and do "the monkey." I followed her advice. I swapped Pop-Tarts for apples and drank water instead of my one true love, Diet Coke. Soon, my whole life changed. The thunder thighs vanished. I had effectively "detoxed."

Many years later, at 37, I suffered another major obstacle: I found myself unemployed for many months. At the same time, my childhood best friend, Gigi, was battling an even bigger problem: advanced cancer. While in treatment, she became obsessed with another personal development guru, the mega-popular Christian pastor, Joel Osteen. Gigi loved Joel Osteen, whose sermons inspired her hope. As a Jewish person and relatively skeptical New Yorker, I wasn't especially inclined to check him out, but I desperately wanted to have something to talk to Gigi about that wasn't unemployment and being broke; plus, I had all that free time. I decided to watch Joel Osteen and, I have to say, he's an exceptionally inspiring speaker.

During a sermon called "Detox Your Mind," Osteen preached that our mindsets (the established set of attitudes held by a person) work just like our bodies do. An overindulged and unaware mindset can be affected by toxic thoughts. Toxic thoughts are anxious, future-projecting or past-obsessing, and catastrophizing—imagining worst-case scenarios. These thoughts are as easy to reach for as a box of sugary cereal and as harmful, too. Left to fester, they will infect our entire lives, affect our attitude and self-image, and become a part of who we are as people. But why?

Joel Osteen said it's because we let those thoughts—limiting belief-laced thoughts, thoughts that maintain and uphold certainty and significance—"take root." He argued that negative or toxic patterns of thinking become self-fulfilling prophecies. In his Texas twang, he said, "When we go around dwelling on the wrong thoughts, thinking about what we can't do, how somebody hurt us, or how we'll never get ahead, those thoughts are toxic. And toxic thoughts left alone become like toxic waste. It gets into your heart, and, eventually, contaminates your whole life."

His message resonated with me profoundly. I know plenty of people who have let their toxic thoughts run away with them. They are bitter, cynical, sour, constantly complaining, stressed, and anxious. I recognized, too, that I had come very close to being among them. Years later, in my coaching practice and through crisis counseling, I observed Osteen was right about toxic thoughts becoming self-fulfilling prophecies in hearing the stories of many clients. Consistent toxic thought patterns, those laced above and around scarcity worldviews, produce dire effects and negative ruts— unhappy relationships, isolation, debt, job-hopping, instability, stagnation, and low self-worth. Just as I'd once scrambled to shed extra weight, learned how to shed it and keep it off with Jane's detox, it was at that point that I considered working to detox from negative thoughts and rise from them, too, so I might shed the extra pounds of negativity that were metaphorically weighing me down.

Gigi ultimately lost her battle with cancer and died that same year. Over the next few years, I would stay, in honor of her, dedicated to my mindset detox, committing myself to reading personal development books: books about happiness, self-love, and even business, money, and productivity. I attended dozens of wellness and self-improvement seminars and hired coach after coach. Over time, absorbing ideas that changed the very way in which I had seen the world and applying them, I became happy. In this way, I credit Gigi and her relentless positivity and obsession with hope for changing many of my stances and outlook in life. She gave me, during our final moments together, a new lease on my own life. And what has been born of it was the protocol I am about to share.

Before we dive in, pause and reflect on your own mindset, the state of your own attitudes, thoughts, and beliefs in this given moment. Perhaps you have let a toxic thought get out of hand. Perhaps you have eaten junk-food thoughts such as, "I can't have it all, I won't forgive this person, there is not enough time to catch up, and everyone else is doing so much better than me" or maybe "This *is* all there is… and it is not good enough." In my practice and in my own life, I have repeatedly seen the damage these thoughts can bring, but the detox protocol ahead works marvels.

The mindset detox focuses on isolating and overcoming five of the most common negative thought patterns I have seen as a coach and counselor and moves you toward undoing them and getting past them. The "toxic five" are **judgment, insecurity (self-judgment), negativity, blame and resentment, and impatience.** Are you ready to break past them? If you are, here is your detox protocol.

1. DETOX FROM JUDGMENT

Judgment is defined in the Oxford dictionary as "the ability to make considered decisions or come to sensible conclusions." As you may recall from Chapter 2, when I responded initially to Scott, the dad in my SoulCycle class, I was responding with judgment and it was anything but "sensible." Judgment is, in most cases, merely stringing together and acting on assumptions, the brain's cognitive shortcuts for getting you to safety. They are, in this sense, nothing but projection and condemnation. Each time we feel a person reprimanding their child in the grocery store is "losing it," we are judging them. Each time we separate ourselves from others on a political basis, making inferences about the "others," we are judging. This is how we live most of our lives; we judge people, judge situations, jump to conclusions, and make assumptions. And we think this is "sensible."

Judgment is commonplace and happens for the reasons detailed and explained by researchers like Daniel Kahneman. You are not a bad person for employing it; yet you *can* do better. If you take the time to change your perspective, you will change your reaction and your experience of life. To shift your perspective and extend your time sitting with uncertainty, use The **Pause Principle.** If you use this, you will see your life take a huge leap.

What you are developing each time you use this mindfulness exercise is **personal agency**—the ability to control behaviors and reactions to circumstances beyond our control, even if these actions appear to be or are limited by someone or something outside of you. It's the "detoxed" state, a state of responsibility, of power, and of wisdom.

A person with a healthy sense of agency believes they are responsible for their thoughts, feelings, and actions. They do not believe they are responsible for the thoughts, feelings, and actions of others, nor do they believe that other people have a controlling influence over their thoughts, feelings, and actions, lessening the impulse to judge almost automatically. When they achieve this, they can navigate life in a different way, releasing unbounded potential and possibilities.

That's why you should achieve this for yourself.

Important disclaimer: Personal agency does not mean you believe you can control the circumstances in your life—you cannot. What you can control is your perspective, your attitude, and your response to your circumstances. You can choose to be proactive rather than defeatist or reactive. That's what this is all about.

2. DETOX FROM NEGATIVITY

Let's do a gut check now for the second toxic thought pattern: negativity. Do you say or think any of the following?

- *The economy is terrible.*
- *I have a thousand emails.*
- *I don't have any time.*
- *I can't afford that.*

If so, then you know these thoughts often snowball, right? What starts as a little negative comment turns into sweeping pronouncements. Pretty soon, you've taken "the economy is terrible" to "I will never be able to get ahead." From there, your thoughts spiral further south—until it feels like the end is near.

This is a common experience (many note it can resemble anxiety), but it is not useful. Pessimism reigns supreme in our culture, media, and academia because it often sounds more intelligent and compelling than optimism. But…is it?

Evolutionary traits, such as the brain's scarcity bias, make us more attentive to pessimistic views. Daniel Kahneman, the renowned psychologist and Nobel laureate, demonstrated how evolutionary traits shape cognitive biases and included among these biases the tendency toward pessimism. His key idea, the brain's scarcity bias, is rooted in evolutionary survival mechanisms because our ancestors were highly attuned to potential threats and scarce resources in a harsh environment. This heightened sensitivity to danger and scarcity has been passed down, making us more attentive to pessimistic views and negative information. This does not mean negative information is in any way more useful to us, however. As Kahneman's book, *Thinking, Fast and Slow*, pointed out, when you think "fast" and err on the side of negativity, you are far more prone to biases and mistakes. If you want to be truly happy and outrageously successful, slow down, recognize this bias, and strive to maintain a balanced perspective on the future.

The great news is you can. For most, negative thoughts are a choice and not practical. They block us from seeing a way through, a way up, and hinder our possibilities. All pessimism comes from a poor choice to focus in the direction of a negative outcome instead of on the equally plausible positive possibility. This is not a good thing and isn't not "realistic" either, as most of the time we catastrophize without concrete, indisputable evidence. Instead, continuing to perpetuate the pattern of negativity, the pattern by which we proclaim that everything is problematic, and then feel compelled to justify just how and why is to commit to remaining stuck in doubt. This can dramatically limit your potential by holding you back from living life to the fullest. Relationships, careers, personal growth, and long-term fulfillment can all be hampered. Not to mention, many people may not wish to sit next to you at dinner parties. If that doesn't matter to you, fine. But if it does and if you truly wish to start "playing to win," then the antidote to negativity lies in learning to do two things:

1. Challenge the "facts" if they are negatively focused.

2. Raise your standards.

First, let's start challenging so-called "facts" and "statistics" merely by challenging them. For example, let's probe the first negative thought: "The economy is awful."

*Is the economy 1 percent "awful?" For **everyone**? Even for Taylor Swift and Jeff Bezos? Forever?*

*Do you know **some** people who are employed, some who are even thriving?*

Isn't it just as likely that there may be a possibility for you to thrive, too?

Is it not true that you have succeeded before despite economic shifts and can do it again?

When you hear yourself making a pessimistic statement, saying something "can't be done," beginning a sentence with "here's the problem with that," or just making definitive declarations such as "there is *no one* to date," ask yourself...*is it true?*

A second way out of negative focus is to raise your standards because, like a superstar, you rise to the occasion. If you decide to go for it, you will get there. You will recognize that your job is to overcome anything in your way, including overwhelm and negativity.

At some point in your life something was important to you, so you went and got it, despite all doubts. Think back to that moment when you made it work. Hold onto that moment. This positivity can even overturn what you think is impossible—like getting over a major illness, losing all that baby weight, getting that major job, or finding your way back into love. You have done this before.

Climbing out of pessimism is extremely useful. Optimism isn't about seeing things in a happy light and thinking everything is okay. Optimism is about being solution-oriented. It is knowing or believing that you can figure it out. Try it. What have you got to lose?

3. DETOX FROM INSECURITY

Insecurity, the third toxic pattern of thought, is a big one. It's the fear of not measuring up, that you are somehow less than everyone else. Throughout your days, some will go your way and some will not. On good days, you love life and think you're pretty great. But then there will be bad days, like when you get fired or when you really let down a friend. Life can bring up lots of fears. Fear of not being liked or loved for who you are. Fear of rejection. Fear that you are not worthy or that other people are better than you. Fear of being hurt. Fear of having to open up and be honest and vulnerable in front of another person. Fear of losing your stability or your job.

This is a normal response. You didn't form your view of yourself by yourself. When you were a baby, you were obsessed with yourself. Your parents, teachers, and the people around you told you who you were, whether you were cute, smart, bad, or not. And guess what? *You listened.*

Today, you don't even need close people to tell you these things. Today, you take these cues straight from strangers on social media! What a mess.

Here's how to turn that ship around and detox from insecurity: Embrace vulnerability. To be vulnerable is to be **honest, which means to stop lying/embellishing/covering up** who you are and what you really want and think even in the face of uncertainty—even when you do not know if people will react favorably or not. The reason you should do this is because vulnerability is the opposite of what you think it is. Admitting who you are, filled with imperfections, is not showing weakness; it is strength. It takes real courage to take off the mask, to be yourself, to talk about things that ask you to reveal your humanity. And the more you do it, the better off you are.

When we allow ourselves to be completely open and vulnerable, we benefit. Our relationships improve, and we may even become more attractive. Moreover, someone who is real and vulnerable gives us the space and permission to be the same. For example: Who is stronger? Michael Phelps, undefeated champion, or Michael Phelps opening up about his struggles with mental illness?

Vulnerability used to be one of my main issues in coaching; my biggest concern was losing face. There are many people who have known me for a long time from my previous corporate, buttoned-up career. When I launched my coaching business, after more than a decade of being strait-laced, it was a risk to put myself out there. For many, it seemed I had lost the farm when I started putting out cheesy, homemade YouTube videos for all to see, but I did it anyway because I knew it was what I truly had to give. Today, people tell me that watching me put myself out there inspired them. When we accept ourselves for who we are—as perfect and as worthy—and do our thing, we start living our most authentic life. And we inspire others to do the same.

When I was 9 years old, we visited the US on vacation, and I went shopping with my mom at a department store. My mom had just had my younger sister and was pushing her around in a stroller, along with a handbag that was filled with jewelry; my mom always carried it with her when traveling. She got distracted and her bag got stolen. Then all hell broke loose. She yelled. She demanded to speak to the manager. The manager could not help her. She accused the store of running a crime ring. Little Keren stood by her side, aghast and worried. When my mom ran out of people to yell at, we went back to our hotel, where she continued to cry.

Hours later, after she calmed down, I watched my mom do something astounding. She sat by the phone (phones were stationary back then), called the operator, asked for the number to that department store, called and asked to speak with the manager, and then apologized to that manager. Yes, she *apologized*. My mom swallowed her pride and admitted that she had misplaced her frustration. That may have been one of the greatest lessons my mother ever taught me. She taught me that acknowledging mistakes is okay. We can ask for forgiveness. This does not make us weak; it makes us strong.

Here are three tips to deepen your embrace of vulnerability and aid the completion of your detox from insecurity.

1. *Drop the comparisons.*

Just because someone is different or has reached a different level does not mean that they are better than you or that you suck. Believing this is like Taylor Swift thinking, "Oh, Beyonce is way better than me." Though they are both musical superstars, one literally has zero to do with the other. Comparison is the fastest way to lose your edge and to suck all the joy out of life. So just don't.

2. *Stop caring about what anyone else thinks about you.*

If you want to achieve any measure of greatness in any realm, including happiness, other people's opinions are a silly thing to consider because they have nothing to do with you. People are never thinking about you or seeing you from your perspective. They are seeing you through their perspective. And since they are not living your life, who cares what they think?

3. *Ditch the self-flagellation.*

In my life, I have been on many diets. Perhaps you have, too, like 42 percent of the US population, according to the CDC. If you are, which do you think is better? Looking in the mirror every morning and saying, "You Fatty McButter Pants! You can never lose weight!" or looking in that mirror and saying, "Hey, good-looking, you're looking even better than yesterday!" The second is better, right?

My father is a master at this. As a kid, I remember seeing him shaving, saying to himself, "You look good today." I recently asked him if he still does that, and he said yes: "In fact, today I told myself I look *really* good."

4. DETOX FROM BLAME AND RESENTMENT

In the vast universe of toxic thoughts, blaming others and being resentful is *actual* poison, which brings us to our fourth toxic pattern: blame and resentment. Case in point: Imagine a couple about to get married, whose divorced parents are still bickering, many years post-separation, about who gets to attend the wedding. Who is being punished in this scenario? The lovely new couple? Or the people who will not let go of resentment? In the grand scheme of things, that blame, regret, and resentment are a far greater blow to anyone's life than any breakup could ever be.

If this is hitting close to home and you are harboring any resentment toward anyone for anything, here are two keys to turning that around.

1. *Rewrite the "victim" story.*

If you are telling a story from your past that makes you feel like a powerless victim, it is keeping you from reaching any semblance of personal agency and precluding you from reaching higher ground. To ascend out of this, you must find a way to look at it differently. Develop a willingness to face the truth with a level of honesty that spreads the responsibility in your direction, too, for it is extremely likely that you played some part in the story. If you do this, you will find some way to accept the story and put it in the past. This is not easy to do, but it is possible. You will find this to be freeing, as it will give you your power back: your power to be in the driver's seat of your life.

Releasing blame is not an admission of defeat; it is the path to freedom. No matter what happened, all the way to trauma and grief, know that you can reframe it in a better way.

2. *Forgiveness*

After getting yourself out of "victim" mode: forgive. Forgiveness is not about letting the other person off the hook. It is about letting *you* off the hook. Holding onto blame and resentment does not give you a better life—forgiveness does. So go on and set yourself free. You do not have to invite them to your next dinner party, but you do have to let it go.

MINI PRACTICE: FORGIVE

Do you need to forgive someone, living or dead? If you do, take 20 minutes and write them a letter. You may send it, you may burn it, but write it out. Forgive them. Forgive them in your heart. Then, let go.

5. DETOX FROM IMPATIENCE

The most common toxic thought running rampant in today's instant-gratification society is impatient thoughts. Thoughts like, "What I want is passing me by," "I can never get ahead," "It's taking too long," "How much longer do I have to work before I have a private jet?"

I get it—you want it all and you want it now. It's not helpful, though. It does not help you get what you want any faster, and it cripples your results. Plus, it completely disconnects you from the glory of the present and from your ability to savor it.

My husband, Ryan, is the person who helped me detox from impatience. Ryan, who is methodical and slow-paced by nature, showed me that demanding a fast climb, or a fast anything, is futile—an anathema to the creation of anything that is worthy. For example, Ryan spends a lot of time in his garden, tending to a variety of plants. Years ago, I asked for a large lemon tree. He bought me what looked like a large pot with dirt in it.

I said, "Ummm, honey? There is no tree there." To which Ryan said, "Yes, there is. The seeds are already planted. It is only a question of time."

Ryan's knowing felt certain. He *knows* that the joy is not in the arrival of the tree. Ryan bought the tree this way so he can grow it, so he doesn't just get some finished product, with nothing to do. He wanted to be a part of the process. Ryan has taught me that just because you can't see it yet does not mean something out there isn't happening.

And today we have a big, beautiful lemon tree.

The Navy SEALs have a saying: "Slow is smooth, smooth is fast." This emphasizes the importance of taking deliberate actions to avoid mistakes and ensure efficiency, even in high-stress situations. This principle is just as relevant in everyday life. Actions driven by impatience often lead to errors because they stem from a sense of urgency rather than necessity. By adopting this mindset, you can achieve better outcomes and avoid the pitfalls of hasty decisions. Which makes this one of the most practical "detoxes" of all.

POSTSCRIPT: GRANDMA'S SECRET

My grandma passed away in late 2018 at the age of 96. (At least we think she was 96. She'd been lying about her age since the 1970s and had even corrected her birth certificate with a pen to keep us guessing.) Before her passing, she was elegant, vibrant, and a party animal every day of her life. She had 10 children and 27 grandchildren. She ruled our family. She was hilarious. She was my hero.

She was 95 the last time I saw her at a family wedding. She was dressed to the nines and tearing up the dance floor. In a moment when we were seated alone, I asked her, "Grandma, what's your secret?" She answered, "I laugh a lot, and I learned to let things go."

This came from a nonagenarian who had lost two husbands and two children, and, as a young widow with eight children, had been left destitute. Yet, mostly, she lived happily, got on with life, and stuck around a long time. On this day, she was dancing. Talk about walking the walk.

I think we would all do well to take my grandma's advice.

Laugh more.

Let things go.

Drop the toxins of doubt, worry, impatience, guilt, jealousy, and resentment. As long as we continue to allow negative thought patterns into our lives, they will continue to take up space and block out the good that can come to us—the peace, joy, passion, and laughter.

Subscribe to the notion of personal agency and believe that you control what you think about, what you choose to allow in. This is extremely useful. We will all experience negative thought patterns, but only you decide how much time and focus you are going to give them.

If you can get through this detox, you are well on your way to hiking that second mountain.

CHAPTER SUMMARY

1. Just as an accumulation of unhealthy food intake can create toxicity in your body so can an accumulation of unhealthy thoughts. These thoughts cause distress and harm, and they can benefit from a "detox," with the aim of loosening them up in order to further expose and eradicate limiting beliefs—for the chance to become happier.

2. The "toxic five" in the mindset detox are judgment, insecurity (self-judgment), negativity, blame and resentment, and impatience.

3. Life's scarcity and negativity have been fueled by chasing the wrong targets. When you choose a new path, you need to remove the negative biases fogging up your windshield. These thoughts are akin to toxins in the body.

4. Toxins can build up in your body. This can wreak havoc on your health. What you may tend to overlook, however, is how your mind is also susceptible to toxicity.

5. Narratives in your head, like "I'm not good enough" or "I will never be successful," are "junk-food thoughts." They may seem banal, but their impact is harsh—and they can get in the way of living a truly authentic and happy life.

6. The mindset detox is a manual for freeing yourself from toxic thoughts. It's accessible to everyone and is an incredible antidote to overwhelm and unhappiness.

CHAPTER 7

Find Your Purpose

*"Follow your bliss and the universe will open doors for you
where there were only walls."*
JOSEPH CAMPBELL

OF ALL THE FEELINGS THAT PLAGUE OVERACHIEVERS, the one that hurts, baffles, and just plain irks the most is the feeling of aimlessness. Anathema to the soul of the momentum-loving striver, the feeling that they have missed their purpose is the biggest of obstacles for overachievers. When an overachiever begins to feel deeply dissatisfied and disengaged at work, like they are missing their full potential, that means all hell is about to break loose.

And, yes, this is a work thing.

Work, defined as "activity involving mental or physical effort done in order to achieve a purpose or result," becomes the lion's share of what defines your life, simply because of the time you spend doing it and the fact that most of life is work (**see definition**). If you don't like what you do or who you do it with, work will cause you the most pain in life. Conversely, if you like or even love what you do, you probably have a pretty good life.

Research indicates there may be a lot of disconnect from loving work and feeling without purpose. According to a study by the ADP Research Institute, 67 percent of people don't like their jobs. That means only about 30 percent of people DO like their jobs, as evidenced by "The Great Resignation" of 2021, with four million

Americans quitting their jobs.[4]

We can do better than that—especially if we are ready to ask for more from life, and many of us are. Before you turn upwards and aim straight at a higher target, it's important to examine what stands in your way in the form of the "disruptions" in your life, meaning any residual and recurring feelings of dissatisfaction to real ongoing crises. When you examine why you may have felt this way, you might find something much more wonderful than what you previously observed. Instead of problems and malaise, you may finally see opportunity.

Knowing what you've learned in this book, it may be easier for you to see why, until now, things have seemed "meh." Many people get swept up in a career that takes its own course, just as they got swept up in unexamined limiting beliefs. You may have fallen into this trap as well. Careers are chosen early, when you are still perhaps under the illusion that you are playing to win, though you are, very unconsciously, playing not to lose. Alas, your bright and shiny career, though you are usually quite aware that it is not what you hoped it would be, becomes comfortable over time. Thanks to your emotional needs (certainty, significance), you become good at managing discomfort instead of pausing to examine it. Eventually, momentum kicks in, the career (like any of your choices) takes on a life of its own, and you stop short of seeing the big picture, chugging along, feeling empty and not entirely knowing why. You watch others pivot into new careers, you wish to chase bigger dreams just like they are, but you feel…caged. And, ultimately, you may end up like the vast majority who stay in the cage.

I can relate. Many years ago, I had a top creative job at the helm of a luxury brand, one of several to span 17 years in an industry for which I discovered a passion from movies like *The Devil Wears Prada*. I felt cool having this prestigious job in a sexy industry. I got to do interesting things like create campaigns for new watches inspired by the great Muhammad Ali, and I got to hang out with stars like Cate Blanchett. (Well, maybe not so much "got to hang out with" as "got to stand near" stars like Cate Blanchett, but *still.*) The point is I had a decent job, it looked good on my resume, and I was pretty good at doing it…but something about it felt off.

Deep down, I had this nagging feeling. Sometimes, it felt like boredom. Sometimes, it felt like jealousy, especially when I was hanging around people who owned their own businesses. Other times, it felt clearer—I knew I felt frustrated

---

4   https://hbr.org/2021/09/who-is-driving-the-great-resignation

with the work itself. It was as if I knew in my bones that I could be doing something more. Possibly for the first time, I began to consider that maybe I had more to offer than what was contained in my super-defined role. As days and months passed, the work felt increasingly like I was doing a bunch of stuff I was good at but nothing that I adored. In accordance, high-stakes projects and moves seemed to elude me, which added to my frustration, even though I only wanted them for a pay raise and title bump. I was constantly asking for more responsibilities and for a seat at the table and, at the same time, being resistant to it and preferring more—not for my resume but for my soul.

Just like the myopia I experienced in that SoulCycle class, I could not see what was really going on. I thought it was my boss or the company, and, occasionally, I thought it might be my qualifications or performance. Spoiler: It wasn't. The dissonance created between my earthly desire and my soul's much bigger desire was caused by selling myself short and ending up in the wrong place.

Had I sold myself short by lying to myself and to others about who I am, what I am good at, and what I truly want?

Yes, I had.

What kind of lies did I tell? The usual:

- *P&Ls? I love 'em. I could look at numbers all day.*
- *Am I organized? You bet. If you want things alphabetized and properly filed, you're looking at exactly the right person.*
- *My only shortcoming? I'd say that's my perfectionism. I don't launch until things are 100% ready.*
- *This job is the pinnacle of my dreams. It's what I have always wanted to be: luxury marketing manager.*

I'd been telling these lies for a decade and never once questioned any of them. I don't begrudge myself these lies today because:

- I often got the job.
- I did try, once I got the job, to work my hardest to keep the lies intact.
- I believed I DID have those strengths.

It got worse, though. I recall once telling a recruiter that I was okay with working on tobacco and fur accounts. ME, a card-carrying member of PETA who, in the fifth grade, staged an intervention to get my dad to quit smoking. In the end, the important thing to know is not what I got away with nor that we all do this, but that those lies really didn't serve me—and yours do not serve you. In evoking lies to secure jobs, I did not just compromise my strengths, I compromised my *purpose*—my ability to find meaning in work and in life. I tried to maximize my weaknesses to get to the top. I was *working against myself*, leaving talent and happiness on the table.

As you know by now, I made a turnaround with my life, pivoting my personal life and career at 40. I went on an inner journey, one that, as a coach, I have distilled into a process of inquiry and a commitment to truth, the process contained in this book. Questioning led me to ask myself what I really wanted, what I loved, and how to bring these things into my life. Any career I'd manufactured out of lies would have missed the mark, the same way we miss the mark when we marry people based on societal checklists instead of who lights up our life. It takes courage to say, even to yourself, "*I want more.*" But you should. All you have to do is *stop lying*.

The ultimate lie is that once you reach a certain point in your career, you will instantly become fulfilled. The minute they hand you that "Lifetime Achievement" award, that's when it will click, right? Sadly, that's not how it works. Take it from me. The second you get the achievement, you're anxious again. A client of mine once called me from an awards ceremony, muttering into the phone, "I don't deserve this."

What is not a lie is that fulfillment and the discovery of your purpose are available to you now. If you're feeling down about yourself or your accomplishments, you must get crystal clear on my five inner-journey questions for discovering your purpose.

The inner-journey questions are:

1. "*What have I always preferred?*"

2. "*What's standing in my way?*" ("*What am I scared of?*")

3. "*What are my passions and why do they matter to me?*"

4. "*How can I appreciate what I have NOW?*"

5. "*How may I serve?*"

Take a moment now to answer each of these.

As you string the answers together, you will be clear on who you are and what your purpose is. Let's take this step by step. Before diving into answering these questions, let's first define what purpose actually is.

THE DEFINITION OF PURPOSE

Purpose is the reason you do or create anything; it provides you with a sense of fulfillment, satisfaction, and meaning. It is your existential why—the reason behind what you do that gives meaning to your life.

How you uncover your purpose is by becoming aware of and fully embracing your preferences and understanding what you love about them. Preferences are anything you have loved (been obsessed with), preferably since childhood, when money or doing what was "safe" did not guide your choices. For example, I love great writing, especially in books and television. I love spending time with animals. I love speaking and communication. These may not immediately translate to "motivational speaker" or "animal rescue founder," but they're what I genuinely prefer to do with my time.

The reason you do what you do is *not* because you are good at it. Instead, you are good at anything because it *matters* to you.

Purpose is NOT:

- A bombastic word that is unattainable. It is not a fuzzy concept.
- Necessarily your legacy. Though Mother Teresa was canonized as a saint for spending her life alleviating the suffering of others, undoubtedly her purpose and greatest motivation and inspiration. The consideration of how our life's work and essence will be viewed after we are dead should not be a concern. Simply put, F your legacy. You will be dead. Instead, care more about the here and now than about beyond our time here.

THE DEFINITION OF HAPPINESS

Happiness is not a fuzzy concept. We know what it is and what it is not, as defined in scientific literature. In the field of positive psychology, Dr. Martin Seligman identified three kinds of happiness, each with a measure of benefit:

1. **Pleasure:** This is what Dr. Seligman calls "Hollywood Happiness." It is the temporary high that comes from acquiring things and achievements. These highs may be delightful but have been found in the study of positive psychology to have almost no impact on your overall life satisfaction, no lasting effects on your wellbeing. So, go ahead, buy that watch and go hang with George Clooney at his villa on Lake Como. Just don't expect it to have any impact on the quality of your life.

2. **Flow:** This is the state of getting lost in a challenge, of losing the sense of time doing work you like and doing activities you love—like reading is for me or watching a great American football game is for my husband Ryan. This state, unlike pleasure, does have a measurable and lasting effect on wellbeing. But it requires you to activate it regularly.

3. **Meaning:** This is the longest-lasting form of happiness. It has the most profound effect in creating not just a comfortable, happy, or pleasurable life but a purposeful life, too. Meaning may sound as abstract a term as happiness, but it is derived from just two sources: gratitude and service. Discover these, and your life will have meaning.

The second and third definitions of happiness above are the new targets. Purpose is aimed directly at fulfillment and meaning and is inextricably linked with happiness. The aim is to venture beyond basic targets of yore—the "Hollywood Happiness"— and toward the longer-lasting and more profound degrees of happiness. This creates a purposeful life of flow and meaning.

Now that your aim is set, we will take five steps to answer the five inner journey questions, which you tackled above, with more precision and clarity.

INNER JOURNEY QUESTION 1: WHAT HAVE I ALWAYS PREFERRED?

The first step in any successful pivot toward purpose: Think *human being*, not *resume*. Many times, we identify with what we do or what we have done, like putting together a resume to present to other people. We find ourselves thinking in traditional boxes because we haven't had many references outside of traditional ones. We live in a society where people ask "What do you do?" at parties. This is why we think in terms of titles, not experiences, preferences, or desires.

There is nothing wrong with that; it's just not the whole picture. Resumes and LinkedIn are about what you've done, not about who you are, what you love, and what it's like to work with and hang out with you. To identify your purpose, you must think about yourself another way. You need to think *human being* by asking about the stuff that isn't on your resume, like who you are, what you love, what your life roles are, and what your formative experiences have been.

Here are some non-resume ways you can imagine yourself described to help you broaden your thinking:

1. **The eulogy:** Think about how you would be described in your eulogy (many, many years from now, of course). This can, though, spill into legacy territory and short circuit overachievers, more often than not.

2. **The sixth date:** How you would describe yourself and your life on an "advanced" date? Not a first date but rather on that sixth date, where there's all the soul-baring, you know? That's a little bit emo, but try it. It works!

3. **The factual:** Just remember who you are. You can do this by describing to yourself and others what you were like as a child.

You have always had natural orientations, passions, and preferences. You'll likely remember that you had a natural inclination toward something that had nothing to do with socio-economic factors like what others were doing, what your parents believed you should be doing, or what type of income you believed you needed for certain standards of living. You just did things because you loved them.

In taking the time to look back, I remembered that long before my glamorous and cutthroat luxury-industry years, I was a chubby and awkward kid with a deep love for books, theater, performing, and people. At my best and happiest, I was in my pajamas writing plays and poems or reading in bed, as if I was constantly recovering from tuberculosis, while my sisters were out playing in the garden. And guess what? I'm still like that! It's just that, for many years, I conditioned myself out of who I really am in order to fit in and succeed. Luckily, I found myself again—the one who loves writing in pajamas in bed.

What were YOU like as a kid? Getting real about who you are is more important than continuously churning out "highlight reels."

On paper or in your journal, answer the following:

What did I like doing as a child, especially when I was in my own world, away from authority figures?[5]

Do I still do those things in any capacity or role in my life (e.g., as a father, a sister, a mom, a son, a Little League coach, an artist, a teacher)?

What you come up with should present a much more "human" picture of how you think and what lights you up.

INNER JOURNEY QUESTION 2: WHAT'S STANDING IN MY WAY?

Changing your work life and upgrading your career will first require a decision: **Stop arguing for the viability of doing what you don't love.**

The mindset obstacle you will have to overcome is: "I want it, but I CAN'T..."

- "I can't be a leader, even though I love my job; this organization won't give me the chance."

---

5   When I was a child, in front of authority figures, I was down to hike and run and play sports. Away from these and left to my own devices, I was a bookworm. This is a very common occurrence, and in order to return to your genuine preferences, remember what you loved and enjoyed when no one was around to monitor you.

- "I can't do what I really want, it's a completely different job. How can I even get to that?"
- "Sure, horse jumping has been my dream since childhood, but I can't dedicate time and money to something useless."

We all have "*I can'ts*." We can shake them off by challenging them. Unleash yourself from the comfort zone and from worry. If you want a life that is meaningful, you have to ask for one; it takes courage and resourcefulness. To some people, the thought "why bother?" will come up, blocking any progress and that's okay. You will find restlessness coming back, as desires seldom pipe down. If you are among those who are ready to live meaningfully NOW, learn to tell the difference between two four-letter words: "can't" and "won't."

Can't is not a real thing. When there is real *passion* and *desire* for something—both words associated with purpose—you will find a way to get what you want. Learn to replace it with WON'T to get clear on who is really blocking your purpose-filled life: **you**.

Here is how I did an extreme career pivot from being a corporate marketing leader to launching an executive coaching and speaking business.

I can't become a coach. I'm too old.

I won't become a coach because I am buying the ridiculous premise that I'm old when, in fact, my whole life is ahead of me.

I can't become a coach because I don't have the knowledge and skills.

I won't become a coach because I am freaking out about a gap I could close with work and study, but I will figure out how to use my strengths toward what I want.

I can't become a coach; I don't have the right strengths profile.

I won't become a coach if I keep buying into this limitation, don't work to reframe, or AIM at what I want.

See? It works. Won't just *sounds* different.

My friend Amir went from can't to won't. Years ago, he owned a very successful catering business with offices all over the world. Yet, at the age of 41, he began to feel pangs of restlessness. He loved his existing business but had grown tired of it. Like most creatives who rise through the ranks, he found himself doing more paperwork than creative work, the very thing that catapulted him to stardom. Then, he remembered that as a child he loved to connect with animals and how he loved sports. In his youth, he always dreamed of horse jumping, but that doesn't pay the bills. It's also expensive and takes a lot of time, so why bother?

Amir decided to bother. He joined a horse-jumping facility and spent so much time on the sport that he sold his business and pivoted his life. He untamed a passion so big, he is now a prize-winning champion rider sponsored by luxury brands. Whenever I see him on the field with the horses, he looks truly happy.

Do what Amir did. Have the courage to *identify what matters most to you, even if it means going against the grain.* His success is reinforced by the Dark Horse Project, a long-term study by Harvard University to understand how people achieve success "by harnessing individuality." The study, instead of wondering the *best* way to succeed, asks, "What is the best way for *you* to achieve success?"[6]

"Dark horses," the study shows, typically don't worry about comparison to others and focus more heavily on their personal ambitions and goals. Translation: You don't have to get paid for what you love to do; just don't use practicalities as an excuse to not even try something you really feel called to do.

To live a life of purpose, stop arguing for what you don't want and figure out what you do want.

What are you dreaming of but keep telling yourself you *can't* have? Take a moment to think about this. Next, flesh it out a bit more. Is this a dream you could get a leg up on if you let go of your doubts and fears and got started?

Let's say you want to be a successful stand-up comedian. Many comedians start out at different stages in their lives, and with genuine talent and the ability to create consistently, they make it. Do the same. Write down the dream: "I want to be a successful stand-up comedian." Next, outline a few examples of comedians who model the success you desire. Look at what they did to get to where they are and then ask yourself what steps you need to take. That's really all it takes to get started.

Little by little, by changing "can't" to "won't," you'll etch away those fears and doubts and let yourself explore something interesting.

---

6   https://www.gse.harvard.edu/ideas/ed-magazine/19/08/follow-dark-horse

INNER JOURNEY QUESTION 3: WHAT ARE MY PASSIONS AND WHY DO THEY MATTER TO ME?

If you have remembered things you used to love and have come up with a big dream for yourself, you may be ready to expand your vision of what's possible for you. You are going to find your *why*—going for the *feeling* that fuels your vision and connects you to true purpose and to meaning. Again, your why is the *reason* you love to do what you love to do. It is the reason your preferences have become your preferences; they're joyful! And often they are in service, since they form the bridge between your gifts and talents and the world.

You can't focus on fulfillment itself to unlock your why. What you can focus on, though, is the dedication to your passions. There is a why behind your love of comedy, your love of color coding, or your love of playing chess. While one person may color-code their books because of Marie Kondo and thought it would look cool, another person may color-code them because their brother is dyslexic and it helps him remember where the books he loves may be found. One motivation is fun but relatively meaningless; the other carries far more meaning and satisfaction than the eye can see.

Therefore, the way to meaning is by focusing on your motivation for your passions, be they comedy, color-coding, or chess. Everyone's got something they love to do and a reason why they love it. Once you find your "thing," you can dig into it to understand what makes it so special to you. That is the clarity you seek.

To get there, ask yourself two questions:

1. *What would I do if nobody paid me?*

2. *Who am I being—for myself and for others—when I pursue this obsession?*

To help answer these, let's break down each one.

What would you do if nobody paid you?

Before answering or reflexively responding with "*I don't know,*" here are two considerations.

1. It doesn't have to be a structured activity, a profitable activity, or even one you think of as "useful." It can just be an honest answer about what you love. As an example, you know what came up for me when I thought about what I loved to do regardless of being paid? **Speaking**. I love the spoken and written word so much that I could talk to a lamppost and would happily spend my days just reading and writing. Today, I'm a professional speaker. As you inquire within yourself about what you do and love easily and naturally, do not worry about what you come up with; just let yourself speak. Bravely name what you love, with no judgments and no worry about what anyone else thinks.

2. If you are still struggling to find what you love, identify what you *don't* love, are *not* obsessed with, and *dislike* doing, even when someone pays you. To uncover what you don't want is still great information. What's great about pointing out what you don't want is that the opposite—what you do want—will likely appear as the path forward for you. For example, if you don't like numbers, you may be a words person. If you dislike working in an office, with a team, you may be better suited for working alone or spending more time out in nature. The more you know what you don't want, the clearer you get about what you do want.

What ultimately matters is that you land on something that you'd like to do. Nothing is too trivial. There are overachievers who have built careers and businesses around barbecue, fly-fishing, and Christmas merely by examining what they no longer wished to spend their lives doing. So can you.

Once you have asked and answered this first question, ask, **Who am I being— for myself and others—when I pursue this obsession?**

This question illustrates that your decisions are about more than just you; they have consequences for your life and on others. That's why you need to know what drives you, what you really love, and who you are when you honor your passion.

Let's go back for a moment to Amir, the horse-jumping champion. His *why* was not to explore a hobby and win championships. His *why* is that, through this sport, he learned who he is: a patient, strong, resilient, mindful person who gives himself the pleasure of pursuing something he wants to do. He unleashes his excellence with animals and with sports, and his creativity and passion for making things beautiful and doing things beautifully.

Whatever you love and truly do with joy, you do to…

- Provide a great life for your family
- Feel loved
- Have a positive impact on the lives of others
- Develop ideas that further humankind

All of these are whys. Whys matter *so much*. As you work to achieve, life happens. Problems come up. If you have a bigger why—a clarity about what you love, why you love it, who you are in its service, and who you are doing it for—stay connected with it. You will stumble along the way without burnout and without failure. Who doesn't want that?

Now, answer the two questions for yourself:
What would I do if nobody paid me?

_____

_____

_____

Who am I being—for myself and for others—when I pursue this obsession?

_____

_____

_____

INNER JOURNEY QUESTION 4: HOW CAN I APPRECIATE WHAT I HAVE NOW?

You already identified some fuel, the preferences through which you experience flow and purpose. Flow is created through activities you engage in that make time seem to stop, those that make you experience long-lasting satisfaction. Think about master chess players playing chess, Ina Garten baking a chocolate cake, or my husband fly-fishing (he *loves* fly-fishing!).

To take it to the next level, add the first component mentioned in the third type of happiness: meaning. The first component of meaning is gratitude.

No one is happy all the time, but you can get there by continuing to walk with the attitude of "focus on the good." Focusing on the good is useful for anchoring yourself in flow, as it is a master emotion—an emotion that overrides all others. When experiencing a sense of appreciation, you will be hard-pressed to feel anything else. Imagine, for instance, that you are on a plane and find yourself seated in a middle seat beside a screaming baby. You might be inclined to get frustrated by the annoying circumstances, but then notice that you're flying safely through the air in a modern marvel, and, to top it all off, you have Wi-Fi and pretzels. Just like that, appreciation and gratitude will take over and the rest of the flight should be a cinch.

Cultivating gratitude becomes the key to accessing and sustaining a sense of flow.

1. Conjure up a positive grateful memory. Close your eyes and take 10 seconds to go on a journey. Go back to where it all began. Do you remember the day you got hired? Do you remember the call that you got the job? Do you remember telling your partner, your friends, and your family about a big win? Conjure that up. Remember the joy, the feeling of pride. Let it stay with you a while. Did you feel that? Yeah. Me, too. I remember my first-ever coaching client. Such deep appreciation comes over me when I think of her. She gave me a chance, and it was exhilarating.

2. Write down three things you appreciate about your job, your life, or this day. Any three things will do, big or small. From being grateful for a client to being grateful for a summer breeze, expressing gratitude for anything and everything changes your focus.

Do this every day. Gratitude is a focus-shifter. The reason it works and the reason so much research[7] has shown that the active and constant practice of gratitude changes your life is because it primes you to look for what you *do* want. Gratitude takes you into focused, winning mode. Try it. You will also find, as you climb into appreciation, that it is an all-encompassing feeling. In other words, when you feel grateful, you cannot feel anything else. Time ceases to exist, and you are in that moment, free.

INNER JOURNEY QUESTION 5: HOW MAY I SERVE?

Martin Luther King, Jr. once posited, "Life's most persistent and urgent question is, 'What are you doing for others?'" The last step in pivoting toward purpose and bringing meaning to your life is to tie what you love and why it matters to a higher cause. In other words, find what you love to do and find a way to contribute this beyond yourself—to others and to the world.

This question is included in a book I love by Tom Rath, *Life's Great Question.* Tom Rath is an author and researcher who spent decades studying how work can improve human health and well-being. His books have sold more than 10 million copies and have appeared on hundreds of global bestseller lists. In his tenth book, *Life's Great Question,* he revealed his personal story. At the age of 15, Rath was diagnosed with a rare condition repeatedly creating tumors in his body. Being a teen, his cells were multiplying fast. Doctors didn't expect him to live a very long life, making the prognosis rather bleak.

Since then, Rath has lived more than 30 years. In his book, he says the biggest gift of his life was knowing, from a very early age, his days here were numbered and could end at any moment. This, he says, got him focused on living life the way he wanted to live it and doing what he wanted to do. The most meaningful thing he could figure out was what his gifts were and how and to whom he could serve.

You don't need a challenging prognosis to begin to do this.

If you are clear on what you are good at, what you love, and what you prefer to do next, tether it to service. Ask yourself, "How can my strengths and purpose serve my family? The world?" That is the Tom Rath hack; the slingshot to Seligman's definition of happiness is to ask and answer life's great question, *"How may I serve?"*

Asking yourself, "How am I best serving others with my strengths?" leads to

---

7   https://www.mindful.org/the-science-of-gratitude/

better days and to more meaningful and enjoyable creations. It really is that simple.

I performed this internal exercise as I began climbing out of my personal haze, wondering how I might best serve others. As I asked that question, I kept coming back to something that happened when I was 18 years old and a soldier in the Israeli Defense Forces. On a bus coming home from my army base (I am from Israel, where military service is mandatory), there was a woman next to me who was sobbing. She was older than I was, possibly 35 or 40. I wanted to help her.

"What's wrong?" I asked.

"Nothing," she told me. I asked her again, very calmly, because she was clearly not okay. She told me her son died—he was only 10 years old. She just couldn't get over the loss.

She had started to write a note that, from what I read over her shoulder, was a suicide note.

Quickly, I came up with a plan to help her. I asked if she had any plans later that day. "No…I don't know…maybe…" she said. Being very young and having absolutely no boundaries, I did not let off.

"Look, my friends and I are going to the movies later. I wonder if you'll join us?" I asked. She did not exactly agree, but she seemed touched and took my phone number. I then declared that I wouldn't go into the movie unless she showed up, basically letting her know that if she did not show up, she was going to ruin my evening. (I have learned these guilt tactics from my mother. Thanks, Mom!). It worked. Reaching the cinema, I sat on the stairs and waited for her. She was exactly on time.

We struck up a friendship that evening, which I later learned was a turning point in her life. She told me she made the decision to stick around because she met one person who cared and was able, even for just a moment, to shift her focus. Sometimes, that's all it takes. This was a turning point in my own life, too. It felt good to apply my special strengths—the gifts of friendliness and gab, and my why—to uplift others. Helping that woman on the bus made me feel good inside, a kind of good that never left me. It was a combination of feeling connected, appreciative, and useful.

Years later, recalling this pivotal moment helped me regain some of that magic. Searching for my purpose, I wondered if there were others who needed to talk to someone ready to speak with them. I found Crisis Text Line—now the largest suicide hotline in the US that's expanded to 15 countries. I joined, got trained, and just showed up. And kept showing up. That experiment changed my life and has brought more meaning than I can ever express.

PRACTICE

- Imagine what you will do/can do with your talent to serve others.
- Then, imagine the faces of those whose lives you will touch through your service.
- If your current approach to feeling fulfilled isn't working, change it.

These three simple keys are your steps to unlocking your purpose. They are easy to put into practice, and you can utilize them again and again. No matter how many times you stumble, remember:

1. Dedicate time for self-reflection.

2. Do something fulfilling each week.

3. Mind your *why*. Connect with it by consciously applying it daily.

4. Have an attitude of gratitude.

5. Serve. Make sure your personal values align with those of your job and your company.

Life is too short to *not* think about your purpose. Bronnie Ware, a palliative care nurse, wrote about death and regrets in her book, *The Top Five Regrets of the Dying*. The most common regret? *I wish I'd had the courage to live a life true to myself, not the life others expected of me.*[8] Connecting to your purpose is connecting to what makes you feel alive. Act on it.

To focus on this sentiment, I end many of my keynote appearances by mentioning the final scene in my favorite musical, *Jersey Boys*, a musical about Frankie Valli and the Four Seasons. In the scene, we see the Four Seasons inducted into the Hall of Fame. When asked what the high point was, Frankie Valli doesn't say "the gold record" or "the fame." For him, the high point was the music itself, the moment they discovered their sound. Like Valli, realize that you came here for creating, not for the creations. You came to achieve, not for the achievements. Let the expansive and joyful journey be the goal now. That's where all the growth, the learning, and the meaning are to be found.

Are you having fun with this yet? The next step will be focusing on a new goal that aligns you with your purpose, along with a concrete action plan. Your new premise: No more goals of the past. Goals of the past were a hustle; they traded your soul's purpose for mediocre gain. They did not come from a place of abundance. They created a relentless pace, limited growth, and exhaustion at the onset of your journey. Instead, attach yourself to a higher goal—one that connects with who you want to become, as opposed to what you want to get. For example, instead of just aiming to be a better trainer, focus on building your own training method and brand. Once you align with who you truly are—an artist, a teacher, a creator, or an uplifter—dump your old obligation/appeasement-bound identity in the river. Find your goal and get excited.

8   https://bronnieware.com/blog/regrets-of-the-dying/

Write down your purpose-aligned goal.

_____

_____

Next, write down five moves, or action steps, you can take in the coming three months to move the needle on this goal. This could be signing up for an accreditation course, reading a book connected to your goal, networking with someone in your field, or, my personal favorite, hiring a coach.

ACTIONS STEPS:

1.

2.

3.

4.

5.

Once you have your action steps, make an agreement with yourself to act on them. And, just like that, you have your initial roadmap out of the gilded cage.

CHAPTER SUMMARY

1. Having a real "why," finding what lights you up, and discovering your purpose is essential to happiness. When you are unclear about this, chances are, you feel aimless, restless, and dissatisfied.

2. Overachievers tend to miss their why by aiming at "legacy" or another status- or certainty-driven agenda. This often leads to choices that send us down dead-end roads that result in midlife crises. Do not conflate purpose with legacy. Purpose is the reason you create, or do, what matters to you. Focus on the here and now.

3. The first key to uncovering purpose is to identify and honor your preferences. The second is to tether it to a service that truly matters to you.

4. Purpose matters because it ends, for good, thinking in a zero-sum (scarcity mindset) way, a way that presumes life's resources are finite, that everything you engage in must carry a tradeoff, and that running for safety is better than betting on yourself.

5. The more you make decisions based on what truly matters to you, the more favorable outcomes will follow. Establish a clear, new goal: the one way forward that will get the ball rolling on living true to your preferences and unique gifts.

To *Really* Live on Purpose, *Really* Stop Lying

"Remember, Jerry, it's not a lie if you believe it."
GEORGE COSTANZA, *SEINFELD*

SO FAR, YOU HAVE GOTTEN CLARITY, a greater sense of your purpose, and a practical guide to goal setting to create a broader and clearer roadmap to your happiest, most fulfilled self. You need one more thing: integrity. Integrity is the quality of being honest even when we stand to bear unwelcome consequences. Here, again, most of us are under the illusion that integrity is something we have. In spades, even. We do not.

Without full honesty, we may get a glimpse of our purpose, but we will fold each time the temptations of certainty and significance rear their heads again, bending us to their will. And if we do get a whiff of our purpose but continue to lie about who we are, what we want, and what we are good at, it ends up costing us much more than our purpose by trapping us in that gilded cage. Therefore, it is worth taking a closer look at lying, and perhaps even making it a friendly image, so we can actually rid ourselves of this terrible, but human, habit.

One of my favorite sitcom characters, other than Frasier Crane, is undoubtedly George Costanza from *Seinfeld,* masterfully portrayed for nine years by Jason Alexander. Short and bald with a massive inferiority complex, George's life was often hilarious and the butt of the joke because he turned average situations and strokes of favor into chaos. Mostly, George got himself into such constant trouble because of his penchant for lying. George lied about everything. One of his funniest recurring lies was about being an architect, a tall tale in which he got entangled, again and again, in various episodes. He also lied about his height and wore special boots with lifts to a wedding, even though they were not appropriate shoes for a wedding. He lied about his elbow moving involuntarily. George lied often—and the results were as funny as they were destructive.

In real life, the results of lying are just as chaotic as George's struggles but not so hilarious. Lies, like mosquito bites, start off tiny and quickly lead to full-fledged inflammation or disease. In the same way, most of us lie to ourselves and others in small ways, thinking nothing of it. From "no, that dress does not make you look fat" to "I would love to sign up for your program, but I just don't have the time" or from "I can't work while the kids are young" to "I do everything right, it's time, money, and metabolism that are the real problems." Our excuses and pleasantries are often lies. Silly, unnecessary, and harmful lies.

You may already be squirming in protest. It's okay. I did, too, when first confronted with the notion that I may not always be truthful. We all like to believe that a few bad apples spoil the virtuous bunch or that white lies are not a bad thing, yet research shows that everyone cheats a little—right up to the point where they lose their sense of integrity and, that in the mental health universe, there is no such thing as a white lie. There is only a betrayal of self, even in the tiniest of instances.

For example, I remember distinctly the two (seemingly) tiny lies that got me into an abusive marriage. The first was when he gave me a bicycle for my birthday. At the time, I was a New Yorker who barely visited Central Park, was not adventurous, and couldn't even really ride a bike. In fact, I am terrified of them. It was also goofy and childish. But instead of thanking him and saying, "Please take it back, I will not use it" and "Don't you know me at all?" I gushed, I thanked him profusely, I bought a helmet and rode all around the park until one day I crashed into a Frenchman who yelled, "You should never ride again!" It was a very *Runaway Bride* act: one so fearful of rejection that it made me compromise the basics of my integrity. And the other lie? Once, at dinner, in the middle of the Bernie Madoff scandal, my then husband said anyone in Madoff's position would have done the same. Instead of taking the automatic gag reflex I felt, using it to get up, toss my drink in his face, and leave forever, I did not say a word. Most lies are like these lies. They are lies of repression, omission, or convenience. Lies are still lies.

In his book *The Honest Truth About Dishonesty*, behavioral economist Dan Ariely took a close look at why people cheat and found that everyone lies (at least a little). Except for a few outliers, this behavior is driven by two opposing motivations: the desire to protect ourselves (preservation of status, circumstances, or reputation) *or* the desire for money and glory. Sadly, the George Costanza small-scale lying is the most harmful. It's the lying involved in constructing a persona—the way you appear to others, maintaining the air of being "nice," "happy," "successful," or of "having it together." Some people lie about their age or their accreditation or will name-drop, while others have a full-fledged persona quite different from who they truly are. They're playing an act, a part, and they're never able to get off stage. This is a miserable way to live.

Some celebrities are known for this sort of disconnect. The late Anthony Bourdain, beloved chef, foodie, and TV host, was known for being so secure and personable wherever he went, but he secretly struggled with imposter syndrome and never felt like he belonged. Tennis star Andre Agassi got so caught up in his façade that he turned to drugs to mask his stress and wore a wig to hide his hair loss.

You don't need to be a celebrity to find yourself living a lie. I have friends who espouse political viewpoints publicly, caught up in the latest hashtags and causes that are, in private, the exact opposite. You think you know someone, but sometimes they don't know their true selves either. Culture seems to demand this of us. Much like poor George Costanza, who so yearned to be seen as an architect because, as he told his friend Jerry Seinfeld, "Nothing is higher than 'architect.'"

If you are lying, consider overcoming the habit, not the merit of your ideology, and the consequences of it. Lying is like perfectionism, which in itself is a lie, a habit that is prevalent and pervasive, as well as exhausting and terrible. Lying can be cognitively depleting, threatening self-worth by preventing you from seeing yourself as a "good" person. It is at odds with what you have learned about lying and requires you to field feelings of guilt. It will keep you chasing the goals but missing the goal post entirely.

Of course, there are external consequences, too. When you are caught in a lie, you don't just trust yourself less and less, but trust in you also erodes in your work and social circles. Lying, if discovered, can hurt your reputation, which means that the looming threat of social ostracism will keep you trapped in maintaining the lie.

The reason it is painful to confront is that we all naturally desire to see ourselves as good and righteous. Once more, the brain is trying to protect you; it would be too painful to realize how often you lie to yourself and to others and how many of us perpetuate even bigger lies: lies of identity. As a result, many of you will find yourself continuing to conjure up bogus excuses for why you can't hit your goals, can't start the business, stay in the relationship, or how going after what you want is much harder easier than lying. If we were to be completely honest, we would be forced to conduct an identity overhaul, and many of us fear this possibility. This, tragically, is how people stay in loveless marriages; tell themselves their career is fine; never admit when they are wrong, lonely, or in pain; and accept subpar conditions for years on end.

Lying is also a massive culprit of wandering around in a muddied state of confusion. You feel disconnected, on edge, or irritable and can't seem to figure out why. Cognitive dissonance is feverishly at work and seemingly unshakeable. This inner turmoil may result in frustration and unease if you don't take heed.

Sudden outbursts of emotional volatility that spring from an irrational part of yourself can point to a tug-of-war between truth and lies. You're doing some run-of-the-mill task and, out of nowhere, tears are streaming down your face. Like insomnia, these physical outbursts are rarely the problem but are instead symptoms of something broader being enacted psychologically. Sometimes, when you aren't truthful about your feelings, thoughts, desires, and shortcomings, your body physically revolts in a dizzying display of attention-getting behavior to alert you. Your conscience is trying to save you, to rattle you enough to listen to yourself for once.

Eventually, with enough starvation from the truth, this perceived balance falls apart because you won't allow yourself to fully get away with it. Much like the saying that a "guilty conscience needs no accuser," refusing to lie to yourself is the kind of self-respect and peace that makes anxiety evaporate. It's a good idea to develop an honest self-reflection practice and to probe your conscience with questions. Ask yourself, "Is that my truth?" **If not**, ask, "Who am I when I do or say this or when I do not say or do this?"

Save yourself the pain and come clean about your motivations or recognize your true wishes. Understand it takes some excavating to remove yourself from the web of lies you've spun to protect yourself. For example, if you tell yourself:

- "I look great. I don't *feel* 50." Yet you *are* 50 and know, inside, that no matter how you look, time is passing.
- "There is no harm in acquiescing to keep my position/status/the peace." When you don't agree, you know, inside, what you actually believe. Which means that acquiescing is not compromising at all.

- "That just wouldn't happen to me. I am above this." You are a human being and can't be 100% sure of anything. What makes you adhere to such a postured position when you hear yourself say such a thing?
- "Yes!" But you actually mean no. Why are you saying yes?

With each of the above, you are lying and you know it. The consequences of digging your heels in and accepting the lies will outrun and outpace you. You can't hide from your own lies. It's very good to face them and to question them. Otherwise, continuing to maintain even these basic lies will wreak havoc on your soul and continue to mess up your results.

You can never escape the consequences of lying because you can never escape yourself. Living truthfully is the only antidote. The case for this, too, was made on *Seinfeld*.

One of the few times George Costanza succeeds is when, in one episode, he decides to do "the opposite" of his usual impulses. Instead of lying, George tells the brutal truth throughout. He tells an attractive woman he has no job and lives with his parents—landing a date with her. He faces off with the manager of the New York Yankees and lands a job with the team. This may be my favorite episode in the show's nine seasons because it makes a poignant point: Though it may seem natural to lie to get what we want, the truth yields far, far better results.

Are you ready to live on purpose? Stop with the lies. All of them. The regular ones and the ones we will talk about next: big lies.

POSTSCRIPT: BIG-TIME LIARS

"Sharks eat well but live a life surrounded by sharks."
NAVAL RAVIKANT

Over the last few years, we have been flooded with tales about those who did not merely lie but swindled for riches: GameStop, Sam Bankman-Fried, Elizabeth Holmes, Bernie Madoff, Adam Neumann, and Anna Delvey (the one who pretended to be a German heiress). They are abhorrent, the characters at the center of these stories, deserving everything that happened to them and that will happen to them.

They are much different than the small-time Costanza-scale liars. Contrary to what you may think, they do not show us fully what it costs to lie because we do not know their internal worlds. (And, let's be honest, most of them are likely psychopaths.) What we can see, however, is that the truth eventually comes to light. For the non-psychopaths in the room, it will nag at us until it does.

I have watched people lie to themselves, to their spouses, to their business partners, and to their teams. On occasion, I have witnessed them doing things to other people and I call them out on it. I'll say, "Hey, I don't think you should do that. Not because you won't get away with it—you probably will get away with it— and not because it's any of my business but because it will hurt you in the end." This is an objective truth. I have no horse in the race and no moral upper hand. My job is to point out the lack of integrity in *your* house that will bring down *your* foundation.

Mark my words, a lack of integrity anywhere will bring the whole thing down. It will happen but not in some karmic, linear, predictable way. No, your conscience will torture you. The worst outcome will be loss of self-respect. You will slowly lose your grit or will self-sabotage. And eventually, you will end up in the chaos you so fear. Again.

It's not worth it. The path of integrity may be harder and longer, but anything in its wake will be and feel good.

PRACTICE: STOP LYING

On what occasion have you lied?

_____

_____

_____

_____

How would you feel if this lie / these lies were to be discovered?

_____

_____

_____

_____

What have these lies cost you?

_____

_____

_____

_____

How can you stop telling this lie/these lies?

_____

_____

_____

_____

CHAPTER SUMMARY

1. We lie to ourselves and to others a lot. This is natural, innocuous, and hard to detect but not helpful. The consequences of this are that you will:

   - Harden yourself to your own desires
   - Cripple your self-awareness
   - Work to uphold the facade, or lie, instead of expending that energy on paths that feel free
   - Grow hostile and mistrusting
   - Self-sabotage your own success

2. There are ways to catch yourself in lies by simply checking yourself and observing your intentions. Working on your sense of worth, too, will help you show up more ready to speak the entire truth.

3. Lying doesn't pay off. Ever. It catches up with you and requires far too much effort to maintain, anyway.

4. Want to stop suffering *and* not lose (get your goals)? Stop lying.

CHAPTER 9

Accept Yourself, Liberate Yourself

"Nothing I accept about myself can be used against me to diminish me."
AUDRE LORDE

Now, THERE ARE REGULAR LIES and then there are Big Lies.

Of all the lies we tell, some of the biggest lies materialize into an entire identity that is somehow disjointed from who we truly are. This may immediately conjure up the images of the big-time liars mentioned before—Madoff and Holmes, for example. But we needn't go so far into the abyss. Big Lies are part of the lives of many of us, as the portrayal of perfection, of impermeability.

You know by now that my facade was a lie, but, a few years back, Instagram and most of my friends and family didn't. Things looked good for me. *Real good.*

Picture it: I was making a decent salary, relatively speaking, at the helm of a glamorous job in the marketing department of a prestigious luxury brand, as evidenced on Insta through many smiles in pictures at work while holding awards or posing with celebrities, occasionally partying with rock stars, too. I was thin and had lots of colorful, expensive outfits that my tall (enough), great-head-of-hair husband would dress to match.

At a restaurant, I once overheard a group of women at the table next to us whisper, "Man, that girl is so lucky." I bet that's how my Instagram followers felt at times, too. #dreamlife.

Except it wasn't a dream. It was a nightmare. Had I known or realized the gravity of my situation, I would have recognized immediately why none of my results pleased me. Had you met me at a gala back then, I never would have told you the truth anyway. The truth was I did not belong at those galas and certainly could not afford the dresses. The truth was that while my then husband flew first class to these galas, I flew coach, about 30 rows behind him. Once, when he asked me to join him in the American Airlines Admirals Club, the staff wouldn't let me in because I didn't have that particular status. Appalled, my husband looked at me as I got rejected from entry and yelled in front of everyone, "You walk around carrying a fancy bag like you're somebody, but you don't even have access to an airport lounge. You're a nobody!"

This was an absolute low point in an already tenuous, difficult, and abusive relationship. The least of my problems was that I was married to someone who seemed to think we should each book our own, separate travel, using separate accounts like we were college roommates.

This was another truth: My marriage, which looked "good" on Instagram, was a complete sham. I was often left alone with the check and abandoned at restaurants around the globe, while my husband stonewalled me for some ridiculous reason. I was humiliated and disparaged in front of friends, usually for my appearance—like a bad manicure being called out or that time I decided to try out the ripped-jeans look. I was told repeatedly that I needed to lose more weight. Once, he locked me in my own bathroom and made threats against my cats. I was alone most of the time. I slept and ate alone, in the library of my house, preferring the television and my cats to any proximity to him. The metaphor of a gilded cage is almost *too* on the nose!

Before getting carried away telling you how awful this was and portraying myself as a perfect victim, I will tell you something else: I chose that marriage and I—knowingly or not—maintained the facade and the Big Lie. I lied along the way in order to "secure" this coveted marital status. I had good reasons. From my mother, from society, I gleaned that marriage was *good* and singlehood was *sad*. Pop culture, fairy tales, and my peers further bombarded me with the message that I was supposed to marry *well* (translation: marry rich). When I married that guy, I thought he was. He was also reasonably tall and had good hair; he looked like the kind of man that would make an impression on Instagram. In all, this would be adequate to my society, and I wouldn't look like a loser any more at friends' weddings.

That marriage was the ultimate *keeping-up-with-the-Joneses* decision of my life. It was a decision I made to fit in, to "do what I was supposed to do" to gain status. Back then, I was obsessed with attaining status. So obsessed that I betrayed all my instincts and said "I do." That might sound like an extreme error to you, something that is not very common at all or perhaps something that could not happen to you. If that's what you think, fine, but check the statistics. Most of us get divorced. Those who entered a bad marriage or made a career choice that resulted in dissatisfaction and burnout have had very good reasons for those choices: In today's society, there is a well-established prestige pathway no matter where you fall on the social spectrum. We all have some measuring up to do. We try to live up to standards and achievements that rank properly next to others. These facts are how millions of bright, hard-working people follow a set trajectory—choosing the "right" jobs, spouses, endeavors—none of which align with true preferences. In time, these choices will create deep, nagging anxiety. Confronted with this anxiety, you may find yourself too entrenched to do anything about it. Many times, you don't do anything. You just keep chugging along. You shouldn't.

As with any form of lying: Just stop. If you are committed to telling the truth, you must also be committed to rebelling against societal values that don't fit you. If you can't show people the real you, then you can't share your struggles and you can't let the light in, let alone go anywhere near living your true purpose.

The way out and up? Self-acceptance. The term self-acceptance is used interchangeably with self-love or self-compassion in specialized literature. Pick your poison. Either way, each of these has been defined in the work of Dr. Kristin Neff, a professor at the University of Texas at Austin, as having three components: self-kindness (i.e., treating yourself with understanding and forgiveness when you feel inadequate), recognition of your humanity (i.e., acknowledgment that people are not perfect and that your experience is individual), and mindfulness (i.e., emotional equanimity and resilience).

To start developing this, it is important to talk about what self-acceptance is *not*. First, self-acceptance is *not self-esteem*. If you are an overachiever, chances are you have self-esteem in spades because you have been working on it all your life. If this is you, you may also be thinking "I know this already" or "That's okay, I've got this." You don't, though—self-esteem is the opposite of self-acceptance; that relentless pursuit is harming you. Here's why: Self-esteem, or what you might call self-confidence, depends on two things. First, your achievements or successes, and second, comparing your achievements to those around you. Do you see the catch here?

The first is that self-esteem is dependent on conditions. The second is that self-esteem has you constantly comparing yourself to others. Finally, self-esteem is only available when you succeed. When you fail, self-esteem deserts you—precisely when you need it most. This is wherein lies the crux. Consider that perhaps you have sought self-love or self-acceptance all along. And before you tell me "No problem, I'll just make sure I always succeed," allow me to chuckle. *You know by now that all you would be sustaining here is the veneer of playing to win when you are continually in the clutches of the terror of losing.*

Self-acceptance is also not self-care. Loving yourself does not mean bubble baths, massages, or flowers (though these things can't hurt). Self-love is understanding and seeing things as they are. This has nothing to do with that massage or downtime you give yourself.

Lastly, though for many, the idea of self-acceptance sounds indulgent, self-love is *not* self-obsession, either. *It's giving navel gazing*, the young people might say. Consider, however, the third element in the definition of self-acceptance—mindfulness and emotional equanimity. Equanimity is chill. It doesn't need to prove anything, which in turn allows you to be less judgmental, less reactive, more empathetic, and of greater service to other people.

Self-acceptance is as practical as it is expansive. Dr. Neff's research shows that if you treat yourself with the same kindness you give others, you feel balanced and live a healthier, happier, *and* more successful life. Also, according to Dr. Neff, self-acceptance can help assuage anxiety and other mental health issues, including depression. Self-acceptance helps you handle adversity and rebound much faster. When you attain this, you will begin in earnest to play to win.

For this to happen, you must reject the notion that you have some "fatal flaw," a reason you do not deserve total happiness. We all have this. Everyone in the world struggles with a deep and fundamental feeling that they are flawed, powerless, or unworthy. This is why, though it is so easy to logically accept that you deserve to be happy, it can be hard to overcome the idea that you have a "fatal flaw" and that you can, and should, fix it—a stance that keeps most of us peddling in scarcity for the majority of our lives.

The "fatal flaw" is an idea we all have about the root cause of our unworthiness, our powerlessness. We attained this in childhood, a period when society and parents informed us how adequate we were: if we were good or bad, if we were pretty or not, if we were as smart as others or less, if we had a lot or a little. What is formed from this understanding of our adequacy vis-à-vis society at large is this idea that if anyone saw the real us, they would reject us.

Every single human on the planet has this feeling to some extent, so don't feel too bad for yourself for always worrying that, at any moment, the other shoe may drop and that things are too good to last, that they will leave you, that some people are "out of your league." Usually, the thing we consider a "fatal flaw" is simple, even silly. For many, it's that they are not as smart as Ivy Leaguers (this appears to me, having coached so many of them, to be especially true for Ivy Leaguers themselves). For me, my idea of being flawed came from remaining single for so long. I believed that only one who was flawed would not be desirable enough to be "chosen" for marriage. When I found myself not married by a certain age (31), I came to believe this devalued me in the eyes of society. (Thanks for that one, Mom.)

This, in a nutshell, is why I ended up marrying such an incompatible soul. Covering up the pain of shame makes us make poor "playing not to lose" choices. In this way, so many people rely on self-esteem—fake confidence, aggrandizement, lying about ourselves—versus embracing and developing true self-acceptance. They're just trying to hide or cover up the flaw instead of digging into the wound and pulling out the thorn, to allow the wound to actually heal.

Consider your own sense of unworthiness so you can overcome it. In your opinion, what is your "fatal flaw?" What is the reason you believe you can't have what you really want? What, if anyone found out, would render you powerless or unlovable? How are you not up to snuff with the Joneses? Is it that you don't have enough money? Is it that you're unattractive? Is it that, deep down, you do not believe you are as smart as other people? Or are incompetent?

Write it down.

Challenge the notion of that flaw from the perspective of love. This perspective will forgive you for being mean to yourself because you learned that whatever you are dealing with or have dealt with is a part of life. Instead of seeing that flaw, try to accept that there is another version of you. There is the version of you that sees no flaws. Find examples of people who have your "flaw" and are rocking it. Find and befriend people who speak openly about their age, take pride in their experience and all the mistakes held within that experience, do not conceal their concerns and do not judge others for mistakes and failure, people who think their curves are hot and that it's okay that we all come in different shapes and sizes, and people who are basically welcoming, generous, and optimistic—and you will find that you always have and always will belong, just as you are.

If you try this, you'll tell yourself it's okay you messed up in that board meeting today; you can try again tomorrow. You are not a terrible mother; you are doing your best. You will also beat the ultimate monster in the face of self-acceptance: perfectionism. More on that soon. For now, become comfortable with yourself because it is the key to genuinely bonding with others. A person walking in true self-love does not tolerate someone who is not just as kind to them as they are to themselves.

Here are some more tools to help you live in greater self-acceptance. These won't happen overnight, but with some practice, they can be developed into a stronger you.

1. GET USED TO TELLING THE TRUTH ABOUT WHO YOU ARE.

Opportunities for honesty present themselves to you every day. Take them. If you're a parent, know that you can exemplify greater strength by showing a child how you deal with a struggle versus trying to look like everything is always awesome. If you're a boss and you messed up, apologize. Take responsibility and show how you will deal with this. Be secure enough to show your true self. Be someone who is real, vulnerable, and at peace with not being perfect. Show up and give others the space and permission to do the same.

2. STOP BEATING YOURSELF UP.

Years ago, Ryan and I went to a very elegant wedding. Estimated cost of said wedding? $200K. For hours, I tried to corner my friend, the bride, to offer gushing congratulations. I found her sitting anxiously—nervously smiling at friends. When I asked her what was going on, she ranted about the tablecloths; they were not the ones she ordered. She wanted the lace, yet she got some "polyblend crap." She demanded to know, "*Who changed the order?!*" She continued, "That was so stupid. I feel betrayed. I feel like I've betrayed myself. You know you really should have helped me. Where the heck were you?"

A lot of people are like this to themselves and about a lot of other silly little things. They're called "perfectionists." From missing a deadline to eating an extra calorie, perfectionists constantly give themselves a hard time over the most mundane things. I coach overachievers and if there's one phenomenon with which I am intimately acquainted, it's this one. I should know, I used to be a bridezilla-type myself, but I have learned to do better.

Perfectionism is never serving you. It is just a chic way of showing how insecure you are. Paul Hewitt, a clinical psychologist and author of the book, *Perfectionism*, likened the inner critic that perfectionists have created to "a nasty adult beating the crap out of a tiny child." Which brings me to this picture, a picture I keep at my desk.

This is me as a baby:

When I see this baby, it's hard to beat myself up. It feels cruel. So I don't.

Can you do the same for yourself?

All it takes is remembering your humanity, that you were once a precious little baby, too.

If you have ever experienced acute social anxiety (worrying what you look like or whether you belong in a social or professional setting), are hyper critical of/ or gossip about others, keep score of pretty much everything (bank account, weight, who returned which favor), watch out for perfectionism. It lurks beneath, and you would do well in speaking kindly to yourself. Unhealthy perfectionism is associated with a fixed mindset (the belief that your basic abilities are unchangeable).

A growth mindset (believing abilities can be developed) shifts you toward *improving* your abilities rather than *proving* them. The former is associated with learning and development, the latter with comparing yourself to others and a fear of failure. This is something Carol Dweck, professor of psychology at Stanford University, has spoken about extensively. The main lesson? Focus on natural ability and avoid labels such as "smart" and "gifted and talented." By doing so, you can see yourself as a work in progress instead of worrying about not being good enough.

3. LEARN TO SELF-SOOTHE.

A lack of self-acceptance and reliance on self-esteem causes a lot of anxiety. What thoughts come up for you in unpleasant situations? Maybe when a date goes badly? Or your partner is being uncooperative? Or your work is not going very well or a client is not responsive?

If your recurring thoughts in situations like these go straight to "They are going to leave me" or "This is so not worth it" and "I must have done something wrong," you need to learn how to replace them. Do this fast before you issue a preemptive strike or get defensive—which many times includes lying.

When something triggers you, learn to calm yourself down. Back away and do whatever you can to relax. Tell yourself, "This may be a moment that I need to get through by watching something funny, talking to a friend, or getting some ice cream."

4. SEEK AND SERVE OTHERS.

When I was younger, not much mattered to me other than making myself happy. This came from lack, from a scarcity mindset, and a worldview that was always scanning the room for competition. Back then I thought that meant succeeding in external ways, like in my physical appearance, financial prosperity, and, of course, marriage. These former illusory aims held me in a gilded cage of my own making.

Years ago, when I began to change my life through coaching and personal development work, I found that to fast-forward past living externally was to shift my focus and live in service of others. I discovered this when I began volunteering on a suicide hotline and taking interest in helping people rather than figuring out what looked best on my resume. It was then, in that endeavor, that I felt my soul begin to soar. Call after call, I developed greater compassion for people, stronger skills at helping those in need, but a much stronger regard for myself. I think that's when I became a real adult.

Dr. Robert Kegan, a former Harvard psychologist, came up with a theory of adult development—a theory that explains how we become real adults. The theory states that adulthood does not merely mean "being able to take care of yourself" but means developing an independent sense of self and gaining traits associated with wisdom and social maturity. Another way to say this is: **Being someone who can also take care of others.** It turns out that real adulthood relies on interdependence, not independence. This can only be achieved through self-awareness and personal agency, as well as through the deepening of self-compassion and empathy.

Kagan posited through his research that about 65 percent of the general population will *never* become high-functioning adults in this way. This majority will arrive at the end of life lacking a true sense of self because so much of what they think, believe, and feel remains dependent on how they believe others experience them.

The reason for this? Transformation is much easier said than done. Transformation means not merely absorbing information but experiencing a "personal Copernican shift" inside our minds. Prior to Copernicus—a Renaissance astronomer— it was thought that the Earth was the center of the solar system. Then Copernicus came along and explained the sun is at the solar system's center. So, while nothing physically changed, the entire conception and perception of the world was transformed. Such is the shift we must experience: We must realize that, although we are still in the same body, that self is not the center of the universe. It never was. My Copernican shift was turning to the service of others, shifting my focus and fixing my gaze upon the collective rather than myself. It has been liberating, to say the least.

Ready to experience this shift? Seek to serve others. Openly offer your gifts to your community and to the greater world. Your life may remain the same after this shift, but the way you *experience and understand* the world will be fundamentally different. This shift toward service will not make you a doormat. The *opposite* is true—your joy and prosperity will expand. Shifting into service and collaboration will take you from 1984 Michael Jordan—playing a solo game, never winning a championship—to 1994 Michael Jordan, the collaborative superstar who won six championships. By 1994, Jordan, who had not won a championship as a solo superstar, was an excellent teammate to Scottie Pippen, Dennis Rodman, the rest of his Chicago Bulls' team, and his coach, Phil Jackson, and *was* winning championships. He quickly became known as the greatest athlete who ever lived.

5. GET SOME HELP.

After my divorce, in addition to shifts brought on through volunteering, my inner life also started to change when I turned to what I'd previously deemed "unacademic:" self-help. Turning to self-help was my first foray into finally admitting that I could use a little assistance, which is particularly painful for those of us in the overachiever camp. It turned my whole world right side up. This book is a testament to all that I learned and serves as an invitation to you, too. If you are ready for the full breadth of work that inspired the book, I hope to one day see you in personal coaching. Anyone can change their life. Including those whose mistakes were broadcast all over the globe.

In 2014, Monica Lewinsky, arguably one of the most infamous women in the world, gave a TED talk about her experience. In it, she lays it out plain and simple: We all judged her horribly for making a mistake.

Listening to that TED talk, I realized Lewinsky was only 22 years old when she interned at the White House. She was only 22 when she was seduced by a man who was much older and very powerful. And she was only 22 when she was condemned by the entire world, through the global news media, for her mistake. (One not made alone, mind you.) Lewinsky revealed that she almost killed herself from the shame, just as many teens today are killing themselves from public shaming and bullying online.

Monica Lewinsky made a mistake. *That is all she did,* and yet her public shaming was so intense that it made her feel like she was undeserving of compassion. I am thrilled to have witnessed, through her talk and her work, that she survived this, turned away from shame and into self-compassion, and turned her life around.

We have all made mistakes. No matter what you think you have done or not done, have or don't have, you deserve compassion. Repeat after me (go ahead, say it loudly, be cheesy):

I accept myself.

I approve of myself.

I deserve peace.

Say these lines often, stop hurting baby you, and if you begin to believe these statements, you will soon find yourself growing up. And then you'll be ready to break up with any anger you have bubbling under the surface. More on that in the next chapter.

CHAPTER SUMMARY

1. Self-love, or self-compassion, is not confidence or self-esteem. They are critically different. Self-esteem depends on your view of your achievements—what you look like, do, or have—and others' views of these, too. In contrast, self-compassion is principally self-forgiveness, the ability to see yourself as an imperfect human and everyone else, too; the ability to speak to yourself lovingly and the chance to stay sustainably equanimous. This is the basis for true power.

2. Self-compassion yields several benefits, including lower levels of anxiety and depression. Self-compassionate people recognize suffering and choose to be kind to themselves, reducing anxiety and related depression. It is also a powerful weapon against perfectionism—an arch-nemesis of the overachiever.

3. Self-compassion is a reliable source of inner strength that confers courage and enhances resilience when faced with adversity. It is the most important "muscle" to master if we are to reach any semblance of inner peace.

4. One of the greatest obstacles to self-compassion is the pursuit of perfection or perfectionism. Perfectionism is not the same as having high standards. High standards do not demand, do not hurt, and do not imprison you. Perfectionism does and is completely unattainable.

5. There are a few ways to combat and overcome perfectionism, including living in service of/and collaborating with others (becoming interdependent rather than independent) and refusing to beat yourself up in your mind any longer.

6. You'll know you've accepted yourself when you handle success and failure with grace and ease and stop lying or putting on a facade. You will feel and be free.

7. No matter what, you are enough, and you deserve peace.

CHAPTER 10

Break Up with Anger

"More evil gets done in the name of righteousness than any other way."
GLEN COOK

SHARP LEFT TURN NOW, but let's go there.

In Munich, during the Olympic Games of 1972, terrorists from the group Black September, a faction of the Palestinian terrorist organization Fatah, murdered 11 Israeli sportsmen and sportswomen—almost the entire Israeli Olympic team. Following the catastrophic attack, Israeli prime minister Golda Meir authorized the operation known today as "Wrath of God." An operation so successful and a story so extraordinary, it has been dramatized in movie after movie (*Munich*, *Golda*) and told and retold in various documentaries. In each version I have seen, Golda's response to the attack is immediate and decisive. In *Golda*, she says, without hesitation, "Send in the boys."

What she means is, "Send in The Mossad."

In case you aren't familiar, The Mossad is Israel's CIA and is responsible for intelligence collection, covert operations, and counterterrorism. In what became one of their most legendary operations, over the next 20 years, The Mossad assassinated each planner of the Munich Massacre and other leading terrorists. The operation, though not without blunders, is still to this day considered a great success. Having been born in Israel, I grew up hearing about it and revering The Mossad. Yet the story never quite really sat well with me. I left the movie theater each time wondering why I didn't quite leave cheering for the clear and decisive appearance of justice served in the end. I guess I couldn't help but wonder: In the end, did this effective operation solve Israel's problems?

The answer, of course, is no. Operation "Wrath of God" was only a success in isolation and with the assumption that momentary justice was the sole aim. It was not a success, *if* you consider that the overall state of the region remains volatile, uncertain, violent, divided, and full of new terrorist groups, and, at the writing of this book in 2024, the situation is worse than ever.

You can argue that this event and the big picture are unrelated, except that big pictures are informed by events. In the end, like the state of Israel, you will find that revenge is not a good, long-term idea. Peace is. If you can choose between justice or revenge—the pursuit of righteous anger, the pursuit of "justice"—and peace, you can, and should, choose peace. Every time. And at all costs.

Radical, I know, but this is another of the profound understandings that has changed my life and that allows my clients to get out of overwhelm, worry, over-work, and chaos, and into the life of peace that they yearn for and deserve.

To ascend into a new state of being you must renounce, more than the chase of money and the addiction to force and hard work, this very impulse to act on anger. Make no mistake, competitive drive is sheer anger; the need to prove something is not an impulse felt by people who are at peace and who know their value.

By suggesting you renounce anger, I don't mean "work out your anger," I mean **break up with it completely**. First, you *will instinctively* do this the more you love yourself. You will increasingly realize that anger, though extremely use-ful for climbing back into power after prolonged periods of feeling helpless, can't help you long term. It's only holding you back and imprisoning your progress. Second, in lieu of anger, get out ahead by loving others and telling the truth. To get clear on whether your actions are about loving, investigate your intention before taking any action by asking yourself, "Am I approaching this from scarcity or from abundance?"

You can also identify the scarcity mindset driving anger and vengeance and work to overcome your resistance to happiness by challenging what is the real truth of any situation before reacting with ire by asking yourself, "What else might be go-ing on?" and "How can this work out better for me and for everyone else involved?" This should start you on a new, more peaceful path.

To break up with anger *completely*, you will have to drop something extremely precious to you: righteousness. **Righteousness** is when you feel you are right, as well as the need to impose that right versus other people's wrongness upon others.

This is strict adherence to what is referred to in this book as "playing not to lose." It is a phenomenon that appears to uphold your position's resistance to another's instead of thinking far, far more broadly or "thinking to win."

Much has been written, researched, and posited about why righteousness is so prevalent. Social media is a good reflection of that because the algorithm *loves* outrage. It's getting worse and even more blatant. In September 2021, *The Wall Street Journal* reported that a Facebook algorithm change sorted the posts that got the most comments: those that provoked the sharpest response. Like other social media platforms, Facebook is trading on our righteousness and our righteous indignity. Indignity is as delicious as sugar.

If an individual or an organization says, supports, or promotes something controversial or that many people find offensive, people swarm—piling on the criticism via social media channels. That post then goes viral because the algorithm is sorting for it. It also goes viral because it is so incendiary; it is making you angry and anger feels great—especially as it brings you emotionally one step up above "victimhood" or "shame."

Accordingly, research has shown that content that sparks an intense, negative emotional response is more likely to go viral. Out of millions of tweets, posts, videos, and articles, social media users are exposed to a mere handful. Platforms write algorithms that curate news feeds to maximize engagement. Social media companies want you to spend as much time as possible on their platforms. Anger is the perfect negative emotion to attract attention and retain engagement. That's how they get you.

Overachievers are more susceptible than others to falling into this trap. Anger is a favorite emotion for competitively driven overachievers. First, because competition is a form of anger. Think about it: If you felt you were already the greatest, would you really feel the need to demonstrate it and prove yourself over and over? In addition, anger is a terrific tonic and mask for fear and insecurity. Many get addicted to feeling offended all the time because it offers a high; being self-righteous and *morally superior* feels good and much better than feeling inferior, attacked, or marginalized. This creates a societal chasm. This may be why many people often refer to overachievers as "elites." It's not a compliment.

In today's state of polarization, many are becoming increasingly uncomfortable with righteousness, both in the righteousness of self and of others. People from all sides of the political spectrum have opposing opinions and that's normal. To feel *slighted* and *indignant* at the opinion of others, however? That's not only unhelpful; *it is intolerable.*

This is one of your final limitations, born of the strife for perfection, to overcome: the penchant to chime in, the reflex of preemptive striking against anyone who might disagree with you, the impulse to land on the purveyor of any low-information opinion out there or even the heathens in your own living room. It takes work to curb this limitation, one that requires focus and discipline using all the tools laid out in this book, most notably The Pause Principle, The Work, self-compassion, and meditation.

Many out there are ready to be done with righteousness. Many are determined to spread more love and compassion than hate and anger. They are eagerly turning off the cable TV news and the incendiary accounts to which they once subscribed and calling out excessive righteousness. Righteous anger strips you of your power to influence and affect true change because it strips you of compassion. Righteousness ends dialogue, ends friendships and careers, and hinders your peace. It is anathema to self-compassion and the empathy you have to feel in order to soar—in order to be free. It is garbage.

Here are two practical ways out of anger, indignity, and swinging your sword at windmills into taking a swing at an inner life that feels good.

1. CONSIDER YOU MIGHT BE WRONG.

No matter who you are or how justified you feel in your values and opinions, consider this: **You could be wrong.** Also, **even if you are right, your peace matters more.**

In my line of work, I come across many worldviews and value systems that are vastly different from my own. Some don't start with the individual but rather with tradition, families, armies, and communities. Some genuinely believe that people should be treated differently according to social status. Some prize order over equality. Some do not believe women to be equal to men. And the harshest of them all? *Some do not like dogs.* (I told you to brace yourself!)

Know this: No matter what side of politics you are on, you are not stupid, you are not evil, and, maybe most importantly, you are not against someone who believes something different from you. To make the most out of the lessons in this book and to truly rise, stop clinging to the false gods of achievement and competition and slide into freedom, love, and abundance instead. Start by questioning and challenging your own beliefs about what is "right" and what is "wrong."

This is especially important for those prone to beginning posts or conversations with the words: "I've done a lot of research on this subject and…"

To paraphrase William Shakespeare's *Hamlet*, "Thou doth protest too much, methinks."

2. LOVE OTHERS MORE THAN YOU HATE THEM.

The second way out of righteousness is to recognize that you may well *be* right but *still* prefer and choose peace and loving others over fighting and mistrust. Pick your battles. Know when to drop it.

To discern between a righteous argument and one that is not, use these three steps.

Step 1: When triggered by someone else's beliefs, before you respond with a hateful or angry comment on their social media, ask yourself, "*Do I have to do this? Do I absolutely need to respond? Would my response really add anything?*"

Step 2: If your brain is still telling you, "*Yes, you must; justice depends on you,*" then ask yourself, "*Do I prefer to post this now, or do I prefer peace?*" If you choose peace, congratulations. At the very least, you are doing your part to not contribute to the ills of algorithms.

Step 3: If you decide to post anyway, have at it. It is fine to comment on something every now and again, as long as you accept that it will rob you of your peace for a while. Do it only if you are prepared for the consequence of losing peace and are truly eager for the conversation.

When you overcome righteousness and trade it for an honest and open debate that does not descend into insults and shaming, you begin to heal yourself—and the whole world.

Note: Recognizing your righteousness is *not* about proving a point or taking a stand. It *is* the expression of your ego with the intention to hurt, coerce, or damage another to help you feel better. Speaking up and speaking truth to power have their place. These acts, which come from integrity, make you leave bad relationships and revolt against wrongful governments. Allowing yourself to express dissent against unfairness is healthy. But overreactions from taking the moves and opinions of others *personally* is unhealthy. Taking things personally can contribute to ulcers, poor relationships, and other malaise. Righteousness often leads to destructive patterns. When you become violent and dehumanize people, reducing them down to that one thing you disagree with, engaging in hateful social media commenting, you are not an arbiter of change. You are just…difficult.

If this resonates, ask yourself: *"What if I made my thoughts a vehicle to be free rather than a vehicle to enslavement?"* There's a fable about this very idea that tells the story of a man rowing down a stream, through fog, and he bumps into another boat. He rails and shouts, cursing the driver of the other boat. When the fog lifts, he realizes no one was even in that boat. The moral of the story is, at the very least, stop yelling into the fog. Not yelling at the fog is the freedom you seek.

Have you read *The Divine Comedy*? It is not really a comedy, but it *is* divine. Written by 12th century spiritual philosopher Dante Alighieri, this timeless fable is about one man's journey through a dark forest to get past Mount Delectable, an illusory paradise, to get to *actual* paradise. Before arriving in paradise, Dante, protagonist of his own work, lands in the Inferno, his creative illustration of Hell—a special place for sins of righteousness. That place is called **the Seventh Circle of Hell**.

Well, isn't it interesting that the *righteous* end up there? In the *worst* place? Also, there's literally almost no way out. *Almost.* Except for one.

Dante explains that the only way out of this circle is to tell the truth, to observe the thoughts that cause suffering, confront them, and then choose the most peaceful option and move on.

The most peaceful option gets you out of the Inferno. Pretty brilliant, huh?

CHAPTER SUMMARY

1. As modern-day spiritual teacher Abraham Hicks says, "A battle against anything is a battle against your own alignment." To live fully is to stop fighting against anything. You must renounce righteousness and its emotional tell: anger.

2. When faced with the choice between justice and peace, choose peace.

3. If you are willing to renounce righteousness and swap it for love, truth, meaning, and curiosity, you will put yourself on a track that has been there, waiting for you to get the life you always wanted to be living.

CHAPTER 11

Pray for a Sh*tstorm

"Hurry up and get everything you ever wanted, so you can start the real work of letting it all go."
CORY MUSCARA

Do you want to remain an overachiever but emerge having read this book as not only more successful but *happier*?

If the answer is yes, you have learned and realized what has been missing. It is, and was, missing meaning, a way of constructing your fulfilling and joyous experience. You have likely gleaned that the secret to mastery of this, of "meaning making," is to roll with change. If you want to live a life of outward success *and* of inner joy and meaning, shed your expectations. *Shedding your expectations is how you roll with change.*

As long as expectations are based on your here and now, meaning they are fixed, you will not successfully leap. Since you will be assuaging the needs for certainty and significance (still!), you will only be able to project short term and will either become too afraid to take all the risks that are needed to truly shift your circumstances, or you will leap and self-sabotage—only to hit a wall again. All disappointment comes from unmet, scarcity-based expectations that are focused on the now and cannot calculate for any unexpected change.

The only way to recalibrate and ensure your success is to do the opposite: Sit back, lean into abundance, release control, and let change happen. Move forward and allow life to unfold in any way that it needs. You are just here for the experience. This should become your new mantra, as embracing change without resistance is the secret to lasting peace and happiness. It's also the truth about life and one you should get on board with. The truth is that *things change.*

The ancient Greek philosopher Heraclitus famously conveyed that stepping into the same river twice is impossible, as both you and the water are in constant flux. This profound notion captures the essence of impermanence: Everything is in a state of perpetual change.

Many overachievers grapple, even here at this late juncture, with a strained relationship with change. After finishing this book, you may still reject, oppose, or strive to control change; you will activate anger again at any semblance of an unexpected shift in your circumstance (bad election outcomes, downturn in business, illness, etc.). Actions you take from this state of defiance or resistance may get you some results but will typically yield a blend of stress, anxiety, burnout, and fatigue. It doesn't have to be this way anymore.

Change can be painful, often causing discomfort, but you have learned that, paired with the right (abundance-focused, self-loving) mindset, it can also serve as a catalyst for personal growth. You are not afforded a choice in this matter; life is inherently characterized by change. It's wise to transition from resistance to making friends with change.

Embracing this perspective acknowledges that the goal of life isn't to evade, combat, or control change but to instead skillfully engage with it. It acknowledges that after a crisis, a downturn, or a big transition, like perhaps whatever you were going through when or before reading this book, a return to the previous state is often infeasible; there are multiple versions of reorder, but the past will never recur.

This shift isn't simple. I'm still inclined toward hard work, planning, and stability, with a position on the stability end of a spectrum (overachieving dies hard). Yet in all the recent years that were filled with tumultuous yet critical change, I realized that the only way to gain real stability was to embrace change. By adopting this new "change-friendly" mindset, I discovered increasing stability even amid unpredictability because the new stability is in accepting the inevitable fact that *things change.*

Scientific evidence underscores that experiencing higher distress during periods of change heightens the risk of illness and decline. Fortunately, the same science affirms that you can grow and become more resilient through change, a process largely influenced by behavior. The time to cultivate these skills is now. Over the years, change has flowed relentlessly, showing no sign of slowing down. As a society, we have grappled with a pandemic and its economic aftermath, reshaping our way of life and work. Amidst the backdrop of widespread social media adoption, the emergence of an even more potent technology—artificial intelligence—looms. On a personal level, we continue to navigate the ebb and flow of life's events: relocations, career transitions, marriages, divorces, health issues, parenthood, and losses.

Now, more than ever, Heraclitus' wisdom holds true: The only constant is change. It's not just that challenges occur with little forewarning within a short span; it's that many events unfold unpredictably. Navigating this new global terrain necessitates resilience and flexibility in equal measure or what Yuval Noah Harari, my favorite historian, refers to simply as "emotional intelligence." Resilience encompasses toughness, determination, and durability—knowing one's core values and standing by them. Flexibility entails consciously adapting to evolving circumstances, bending without breaking, and evolving even to the extent of altering viewpoints. This fusion of qualities cultivates a sturdy endurance, sustaining one's core even in fragile moments. It enables you to embrace the world's natural cycle of order, disorder, and reorder—a dance akin to Heraclitus' river. Through this approach, you stand a chance to skillfully navigate change, reaping its benefits whenever possible, and the chance to shield yourself by what's starting to look like an unbearable onslaught of increased stress.

And what if you can't drop expectations and roll with change like it's nothing, at least not right away? Don't worry, life will drop them for you, through some difficult turn of events. That's just life. I don't hope it does, but I know by now that this moment will come to all of our doors. In every person's life, there will come a point where problems pile up so high, they can no longer ignore them, or there will arrive a wall that will stop everything in the form of a traumatic event.

If you are seeking real enlightenment, true freedom, you will be prepared for this moment and come through it. You may even recognize that you need it. Many people need a "storm" to get moving and face the truth. At the end of their coaching journeys, for example, some of my clients make it all the way to the doorway to freedom—the edge of the cliff—but, just before they jump, they balk, often preferring to remain pure potential. "Should I stay or should I go?" This is the common question asked here. Like they're bargaining with me or something.

That's when a storm comes in really handy. It makes the decision for you. In this way, it may feel awful, but it's not a bad thing at all.

The promise held in this book is grand, but I have also been honest with you: Side effects come with the shedding of the old self. It takes immense courage to jump onto a path that is truer for you. Now that you stand at the precipice, you may be tempted to just shrug and say, "No, thanks" and stay where you are.

If you've read this far, you'll unlikely turn back. The desires and excitement within you are not going to subside after you close this book; they will get louder. You can reason with yourself and realize it's far less scary to jump than to stay stuck somewhere that doesn't suit you. You can also lose the fear by recognizing that in asking for certainty you are bargaining with the devil because there is no such thing as certainty.

Here are four next steps you can take to charge at a new start, even with no semblance of certainty:

1. **Stop making excuses and accept that starting over is essential.** You often get stuck in life because you're either unable or unwilling to accept your reality as it is. Instead, you stubbornly continue to indulge in the fantasy of how you wish things were. Get real with yourself. Ask, "What's my situation now? How can I work with what is, not what I wish it was?" With a dash of honesty, you may conclude that things are not that great, and you are better off rolling with the tides of change rather than staying stuck. Don't stay stuck. Start over.

2. **Make a decision.** Now that you have some ideas for possible paths you could take that fall in line with your values, it's time to decide. Which one will you choose? "Decision" comes from the Latin word *decisio*, which literally means "to cut off." While picking one path means cutting yourself off from all others, it doesn't mean that you can't course-correct later by choosing a different one if things don't work out or feel right. Just make the right decision for right now.

3. **Get planning.** Planning is how you create some semblance of being sure-footed. It still won't be certain, but you feel better with a clear vision and a concise plan. The process of rebuilding your life from the ground up won't be easy, but having a plan will greatly increase your chances of carving out the life you want successfully. To begin, revisit Chapter 7 and the goal you wrote out at the end of it. Does this goal still seem pertinent to you, like the one thing around which you would like to center your desire and genius? If so, make a list of 20 action steps you can take to make that goal a reality in the next three to six months. Once this has been written, review your list, editing and eliminating the steps

that are not 100% for you. Then, take the ones that remain, put them on the calendar, and get moving.

4.   **Surround yourself with role models and mentors (like a great coach).** When you're trying to rebuild a new foundation for your life (preferably a rock-solid one), you'll need some guidance from a mentor. This could be someone who has achieved a goal you've set your sights on, has reinvented themselves successfully, or just has the qualities you're working toward building within yourself. They don't have to be someone you know personally. My mentors have included some of the best coaches in the world and Madonna and Yuval Noah Harari, with whom sadly I do not personally hang...yet. Watching them do what they do inspires me. Yours will inspire you to do more—and do it better. You will also feel less alone as you brave the wilderness.

Take some extra time here, sitting with the ideas and collecting your strength for the path and sh*tstorm ahead. When you are ready to cross that chasm, you will cross it with enthusiasm.

PRACTICE: CHANGE YOUR QUESTIONS, CHANGE YOUR OUTCOMES

The fault in our expectations lies in *how* we ask things. Usually, because we are trying to "solve" for something (based on the flawed, underlying premise that "something" will lead to happiness), we ask closed questions, such as: "How can I get a million dollars?" or "How can I get more clients?" or "How can I get them to change?"

Such questions are rife with expectations. They will fail you. To lean into abundance, let light in and roll with change. Here are two open-ended questions you can ask instead.

1. *What would it take for this thing I want to show up?*

This question leaves far more room for options and possibilities, and for allowing forces other than your own sheer will to bring you what you want.

2. *How can this work out well for me?*

This question also leaves the end open but also importantly presupposes there is a way all that is happening ends well. Change will likely be welcomed, not feared.

In the long run, you will realize that a storm—any storm, any change—may be the best thing that can happen to you. It all depends on your perspective. Whether you believe the storm is coming or not, it can't hurt to have an umbrella.

CHAPTER SUMMARY

1. Change is life; embrace it. Resisting truth is what leads to stress, anxiety, and dissatisfaction. Instead, embracing change with an abundance-focused, self-loving mindset can lead to personal growth and fulfillment.

2. Adopt not just an abundant mindset but an "allostatic mindset:" The concept of allostasis suggests that stability is achieved through dynamic equilibrium, adapting to change rather than resisting it. It emphasizes the importance of continually rewiring the brain and forging new connections to maintain stability amid change.

3. The keys to lasting, sustainable joy and success are resilience and flexibility. Developing emotional intelligence, which includes resilience and flexibility, is crucial for navigating change successfully. Resilience involves toughness, determination, and standing by core values, while flexibility entails adapting to evolving circumstances.

4. Want to be *really* happy? Let go of expectations. Expectations (having an agenda of any kind) are based on scarcity. Focusing solely on these, your path to fulfillment can lead to disappointment, as it is once again a submission of your power to external forces. Instead, adopting open-ended questions and letting go of rigid expectations allows for greater flexibility and adaptability in the face of change.

5. When you feel ready, take action. Taking proactive steps, such as accepting reality, making decisions from abundance, making plans, making hires, making a move, and seeking guidance from mentors, can empower you to navigate change and build a life you truly love from this point on.

I bet you are excited to get going and climb that second mountain now. Let me know how you like the view.

CHAPTER 12

Step into Your Authentic Power

*"Authentic power is the energy that is formed by the intentions of the Soul.
It is the light shaped by the intentions of love and compassion
guided by wisdom."*

GARY ZUKAV

WHEN I FIRST MEET A NEW CLIENT, many tell me the ways they are powerless—not directly but by alluding to a lack of control. They say things like, "He made me so angry," "The kid is driving me crazy," "They did that to me," "The environment here is toxic," or even "It's all not working, I can never get ahead," followed by a barrage of circumstances somehow seen as insurmountable. What this boils down to is a sense that the world is doing things *to* them.

Perhaps that is how you felt when you first opened this book: the opposite of personal agency.

Now you are on the other side, about to exit the Inferno, probably feeling clearer about yourself and feeling armed with personal agency and with new ideas that will move you forward and that make the expression of powerlessness far less tolerable. You are about to notice just how many people around *you* express powerlessness or demonstrate the scarcity mindset. And it will likely annoy you.

You may have moved ahead; they have not. One impulse may be to coax them or even "educate" them into your new, enlightened position. You may even give this book to everyone you know (I honestly hope you will). You may start talking people's ears off about your epiphanies. If you do, many will thank you, but others will not be ready for the information, will not implement even the simplest of

GILDED

mindfulness techniques offered, and will not be inspired to set their lives ablaze by dropping all the lying and posturing. They may even question your judgment and duck behind sofas when you enter a room to avoid you.

When this happens (it 100% will), you do not get to blame them, nag them, argue with them, or condemn them. That only offers them more righteousness, denying you of any authentic power. To remain in resistance is to continue to "play not to lose." Nor do you get to turn back. If you are ready to truly ascend, you must head full throttle for the home stretch and cultivate your ability to walk fully in your power. This chapter will show you the way.

Awareness of why you still think in any judgmental way versus practicing mindfulness (slow, proper thinking) can get you out of the feeling that life is happening *to* you, as well as of the thought that *they* are an affront. If you cannot reach this discernment, you will continue to feel that you must assert yourself and use action and force to create power. Assertion or force will attract more assertion. People are going to meet you with equal force and resist you, stripping you of any influence. Life will feel like a continuous struggle.

Authentic power simply means employing all the positive thinking you have learned here and exercising greater inner control. In a viral video known as the "Mind of the Athlete," a speaker introduces a tennis academy study conducted in Florida, aimed to differentiate top-five-ranked tennis players from those ranked between sixth through twenty-fifth. Surprisingly, factors like diet, exercise, starting age, and coaching were insignificant to top rankers. It was found that top player' engagement in positive or proactive thinking in the moments following a point made all the difference. Thoughts such as "I love this game" or "I'll get the next one" led to decreased heart and breathing rates. This positive mindset and improved physical condition enabled top athletes to conserve energy, boost their self-confidence, and secure victories. Ultimately, less effort, more positive, abundance-minded focus achieves the real gold.

The bottom line of this book, if there is one, is that anything you create by finding clarity and equanimity creates infinitely better circumstances than paltry flexing ever will. This is *authentic power.*

A client of mine wanted a new job. Out of the workforce for five years after having a baby, she had quit and survived a "soul-sucking job" before then. When we met, she'd been searching day and night for a new job. She sent resumes everywhere. She called every friend she could think of and had several job interviews. So far, so good. However, when push came to shove, she kept "blowing it." Each time she got an interview, my client locked herself into the belief that this opportunity was *the one.* In her growing desperation, she idolized any position as the "optimal position." She obsessed about hearing back and followed up with solicitous and perhaps a little overzealous energy. She fantasized about how this job would be her salvation and talked that way. The result? The interviews went nowhere, until she realized that her zeal was causing her to use force and not power. Force repels. Power compels.

Neediness never comes from power. Neediness comes from insecurity, doubt, or lack or from the scarcity mindset. This kind of energy, the energetic projection of your powerlessness and your desperation to "close the gap" is always working against you, and it causes you to exert way, way, way too much force. Force that, like anyone arriving on a date with a timeline for marriage, is a red flag for anyone on the receiving end.

You will not complete this journey until you learn to not only drop the righteousness but earnestly chill and allow life to come to you instead of barreling at it like Michael Jordan at the basket in the 1990s. Dropping the force takes some getting used to, but you will see it works. When my job-seeking client realized her neediness was sabotaging her efforts, she changed her approach. She softened up and started to understand that she was much more attractive as a hire when she was eager and earnest. From that point on, she went to job interviews more determined to see if they were right for *her* rather than how she could comply with them. To assuage the "necessity" that she felt around this ordeal further, my client also bought herself some time and financial peace of mind by doing odd jobs on the side so that money and urgency were less of an issue, allowing her to be even more relaxed as she approached her search. In time, space opened for just the right opportunity to come through.

If you are an overachiever ready to fully transform your life, walk in your authentic power—devoid of judgment, lying, fraud, self-betrayal, negativity, resentment, impatience, coercion, righteousness, and *effort, too.* Authentic power is staying in power and is founded upon the ability to distinguish love versus fear and to approach any power struggle from love by using mindfulness tools such as The Pause Principle. These will make you feel calmer, and a calm and decisive energy reigns supreme.

Inner or authentic power, in contrast to force (external power), will be easy for you to categorize now. The distinction will resolve the need to suffer unnecessarily again because the cost (maintaining force, constantly proving yourself, working very hard) is too high a price to pay in this life for anything. As we have said, the maintenance mode may have yielded for you and continue to yield **external power**, such as helping you get the corner office, more money, and more status. However, this is a facsimile of power and is the least powerful form of power. Even worse, this only keeps you "playing not to lose."

Each accomplishment derived from external power is a bastion of force, putting on a mighty front, making it vulnerable, combustible, and unsustainable. Their actual power is finite and is extremely fickle because it depends on conditions. Upholding these depends on the ability to manipulate and control; it is destructive, depending on a constant battle against the feeling of powerlessness. Authentic power is the ability to trust yourself, to stop scarcity thinking, and to continue to expect that things will turn out abundant.

Now would be a good time to go back to Chapter 5 and revisit the emotional scale. Feel within yourself which are low and indicative of force versus those that are higher and indicative of authentic power. Here's the scale again.

LOWER EMOTIONS	HIGHER EMOTIONS
certainty and significance	love and growth

1. fear	1. calm
2. shame	2. hope
3. blame	3. peace
4. resentment	4. eagerness
5. regret	5. enthusiasm
6. defiance	6. joy
7. frustration	7. excitement
8. anger	8. gratitude/appreciation
9. defensiveness	9. acceptance
10. craving/obsessive desire	

Each time we try hard, argue with people, work ourselves to the bone and into states of frenzy and overwhelm, we are operating from the lower emotions and are sending a signal to our souls that we are not enough, that we are separate from them. Often, as the addiction to using force is so powerful, we continue to tell ourselves that trying hard is noble. This is not true; it's just how we have been conditioned. We learned early in life that if we just plead our case to mother, mother will give us a cookie. When we were children, sometimes this worked and we got our cookie.

The universe is not your mother. If it sees you begging and using force, it will send more begging and force right back atcha.

Internalize that solicitation is from now on unworthy of *you*. You will move swiftly away from this low-level default and start playing to win, simply by doing two things from here on out:

- First, surrender a big part of your ego identity—the person who "has" to work very, very hard to get anything.
- Second, gauge what authentic power emotionally corresponds to versus what force corresponds to and refer to the emotional scale.

Start to understand how to gauge whether you're in a state of force (a state of resistance, also called "interference") and when you're in a state of power (one of non-resistance, also called "non-interference"). In interference, it doesn't matter how many awards, accolades, and sums of money are thrown your way; you will find a way to mess it up. You won't be able to hold onto it because it'll feel wrong. You'll be like, "I don't deserve this seven-figure deal or this great boundless love. So I'm going to freak out and worry about how to demonstrate my merit to these investors and how to pay them back or to scare the lover away with my incessant controlling and neediness."

This is not a good path for long-term success, ease, or happiness. So, instead of channeling Elon Musk (*Mr. Desperado*) or Adam Neumann (*Mr. Bravado*), channel Warren Buffet, a friendly old man who really only sees in very long swaths of time and is allowing himself to move through it, slowly like a big whale collecting fish along the way, knowing he doesn't have to go after the fish but merely open his mouth…occasionally.

It's now or never. Ask yourself, "Am I 100% ready to TRULY live?" If so, embrace your authentic power and leave force behind.

Using force is doomed, anyway.

To come of age is to humbly understand that we are here for a brief moment and should relish, to relinquish all force, blame, narratives that cast us as powerless, and from there allow ourselves to live fully in this brief time with *any* of the accouterments we want—but only if they are begotten with a side of joy and ease.

If that sounds good to you, you are ready to leave the Inferno.

THE TEST: WHAT TO EXPECT WHEN YOU *REALLY* SUCCEED

"When you do well you become a sign of hope to the optimists, but to the pessimists you represent the stink of their own failure."
GUS PORTOKALOS, MY BIG FAT GREEK WEDDING 2

Wondering what you can expect once authentic power becomes your MO? Conflict. And lots of it. Most people will stay where they are, and if they have gotten accustomed to a former version of you who postured and acquiesced to please them, now that you emerge powerful, knowing who you are and what you want, they will not like it, and they will react in disapproving ways. For example, one of my favorite teachers, Martha Beck, author of *The Way of Integrity*, faced divorce and excommunication from the Mormon Church after her "truth cleanse" and decision to rise; she was rejected by her religion, her society, her people. All of them. I did not experience anything that extreme but did lose many of my social-climbing friends and went through many other travails on the road to just being myself. You can expect this, too.

What to do here? I have three tips for you, each of which can and will only follow true self-compassion. If you are still playing "not to lose," you can forget about them.

1. Develop and uphold real boundaries. People will criticize you, people will adore you, people will gossip about you, and people will want things from you. Your job will be to drop your former "disease to please," not acquiesce because you want people to like you and engage with clear boundaries (honesty). As Brené Brown famously says in her book, *Dare to Lead*, "clear is kind." Be clear about who you are, where you are going, what is comfortable for you, and what is not aligned with your values. Only by maintaining real boundaries can you succeed, this time with fulfillment.

2. Make much less effort to explain yourself. Do not underestimate your desire to continue to "line up" with your old crew and with your family of origin. As you rise, however, you will suffer breakage from many of these people, who will either flat out take leave from your life or find fault with what you are choosing to do and how you are choosing to do it. The temptation to explain yourself, share everything, and fire back at their commentary may be extraordinary, but…don't. Go forth and rise. They will all reappear. As Taylor Swift once quipped in an interview, "There will be no further explanation. There will just be reputation."

3. Work less. As William Penn quipped, "Time is what we want most, but what we use worst," so this one is really important if you wish to "play to win." Though you may believe that your overwork impulse comes from your innate industriousness, it does not. It comes from futile adherence to a pace that is likely not your own. Challenge this and any other notion of "success" you have come to adopt as gospel. Who knows? It may not be for you after all. And if it is not, there is another way.

Ask yourself, "How would I work if I truly believed in my endeavor? What would I show up for? Wouldn't I give myself a break, enjoy long stretches of time each day for reflection, show up joyfully to my important tasks, and leave the desk when creativity is no longer available?"

You may find in answering these questions and in offering yourself compassion, that this shall suffice to end the obsession with busyness and pleasing society and give way, at last, to excellence.

POSTSCRIPT: EXODUS

"We must let go of the life we have planned, so as to accept the one that is waiting for us."
JOSEPH CAMPBELL

My favorite episode of *Frasier* is the first episode of the sixth season, which aired in 1998, called "The Good Grief." In it, Frasier Crane, played by Kelsey Grammer, has been fired from his prestigious job as the host of a successful radio show and is struggling with becoming gainfully employed again. Frasier deals with the loss of his job and the "in-between" period of uncertainty as though he were experiencing the loss of a loved one, moving through the five traditional stages: denial, anger, bargaining, grief, and acceptance, each with some weird results. In between job hunting, Frasier keeps himself busy by hosting a picnic for the other unemployed staff, writing an opera, assembling his "fan club" (only to realize there are only three members), and generally annoying everyone he encounters with his new, overzealous attitude of complete and utter denial.

Niles, his brother, played by David Hyde Pearce, is also a psychiatrist and, observing this, accurately diagnoses that Frasier, like any overachiever whose identity is tied to his work, is grieving. To help Frasier deal with the emotions that will allow him to exit the stage of denial and cycle through the stages of grief, he gives him a nudge over the edge by saying, "Frasier, you're not famous anymore!"

At this, Frasier (hilariously) finally lets go of the farce and breaks down sobbing. Finally, in admitting defeat and being able to access depression, he can begin to shed the old self, which is the only way to reach the last stage of grief: acceptance.

In watching it (again and again), I have learned and appreciated this flawless analogy for any transition: Without going through grief, you do not fully let go (of righteousness, of lying, of force, of former identities) and move forward. You stay in purgatory. You must deal with grief to close the door fully before moving to a new chapter. And to do that, you will need to come to terms with the feelings. If you are experiencing any of these, even if you have not yet taken a single step beyond reading this book, allow yourself to feel the feelings. Denial. Anger. Bargaining. Sadness. Acceptance. Take time to grieve.

You are burying an old self when you decide to go on the inner journey. You are saying goodbye to an era of your life and to a former definition of yourself.

The only way to move forward is to let go. Like Frasier, grieve the loss, for what's gone is gone. In time, the emotions will run their course, new circumstances will set in, and you will get a chance to move forward like never before.

PRACTICE: PUT IT DOWN

Picture yourself going through a very busy airport like JFK. Like life, it's all hustle and bustle and noise. Now, imagine you are carrying luggage. A lot of luggage. It's heavy, and it is old-school, meaning it doesn't have wheels. You're carrying all this heavy luggage, each suitcase containing garbage that's weighing you down. In one suitcase there is fear and doubt. In another, anxiety and worry that you're a fraud and nobody really loves you. In another, analysis paralysis. In another, blame and resentment. In yet another (how are you even holding yourself up all this time?): judgment of yourself, of the past, of others.

Then, you realize, "I can put the suitcases down."

Now, visualize putting each suitcase down—plunk!—on the ground.

And when they are all down, imagine realizing you really don't need anything in those suitcases where you're going.

Leave them behind: all the angst, the internal pressure to overachieve, the overwhelm born of inauthenticity, the burden of keeping up all those appearances. Take only a small carry-on filled with eagerness and spiritual support. That's all you're going to need where you're going. This is what authentic power feels like: no baggage, no extra weight. This metaphorical removal makes a point: You don't need to carry extra weight.

Put in spiritual terms: *Suffering is optional.* This is not a permanent understanding, but once reached, you can come back whenever you like, and your choices will feel…well, like a choice.

CHAPTER SUMMARY

1. Authentic power is "power to" and "power with," not "power over." It depends on no conditions, places no blame on conditions, nor asks for control.

2. When you live to serve your soul—whose harmonious intentions are interested in meaning and happiness—you are the interpreter of meaning and can sort through your circumstances. That's authentic power.

3. Authentic power, power from within, seeks and needs far less validation. This is when you will begin to meet the most conflict from others who do not feel as elated or as enlightened as you. With boundaries and with far less need to explain yourself, you will develop a new way to engage with them and rise even further.

4. You can also drop any residual baggage now, too. You don't have to carry your whole life's suffering and trauma to the next level. Your new identity, one more committed to happiness and freedom than to surrogates for certainty and significance, does not require it anymore. Enlightenment does not ask you to bring it with you, either. You have agency and can metaphorically release it or "put it down."

5. Strive to live suffering-free. Recognizing this will feel lighter. This is the beginning of ascension.

Welcome home.

From Restless Swan to Wild Goose

*"Stop trying to feel good. **Be** good."*
COACH KEREN, AUTHOR OF THE VERY BOOK IN YOUR HANDS

WELL, HERE WE ARE, SUPERSTAR. You did it! The inner journey you've embarked on is truly a life-changing trip, and this segment of yours is, for now, complete. I'm honored that, of all trips in this lifetime, you chose to take this one with me. It is a privilege I never take for granted.

There's a poem by Mary Oliver that I keep going back to called "Wild Geese." It's about finding comfort and freedom in nature and in our own nature while the world goes on. In Oliver's verse, wild geese are representative of those who do just that: They move swiftly on, with the seasons, with life. For copyright reasons, I cannot share this poem here with you but encourage you to look it up and read it. In summation of this book, I encourage you to come to heed her sentiment; think of yourself never again as a swan and ever more as a goose.

Swans are not only far bigger than geese and therefore at risk of drowning beneath their plumage, they are also highly territorial and very aggressive. Geese, in contrast, are smaller and nimbler on the water, and, as a species, mind their own business, acting in defense only when their nest is directly attacked. Employing Oliver's poem, we have an alternative: to be nimble as a goose and true to our lighter nature. The metaphor is complete.

Should you ever need a quick refresher of the ideas you've gleaned through this book that will help you stay true to your lighter nature, here are a few takeaways:

1. Stop leaping to limiting beliefs that keep you blocked. Let go of fake certainty so you can finally control 100% of your destiny. You get to create the life you want.

2. Employ The Pause Principle on the regular and you'll be living in abundance—making the most out of every circumstance.

3. Focus more on maximizing pleasure and happiness. Watch what this does to your life.

4. Stay in integrity. Tell the truth. Operate from abundance so you lose your fear and find the right way ahead. This is how you play to win.

5. Love yourself first. When you approve of yourself, forgive yourself, give yourself compassion and a little credit, you will show up differently in your life.

6. Follow your bliss and be happy. Do what makes your heart sing. This is not advice that is reserved just for people like Taylor Swift. It's for you, too.

7. Contribute beyond yourself. Give with both hands at every turn without expecting credit. It is far more effective to *be* good than it is to try to feel good. Do good = feel good.

With that, you've reached the end of the road. It sure has been a journey together, hasn't it? Thank you for not only reading this book but for challenging yourself to think differently and let those old patterns, behaviors, and mindsets go.

If you feel like you want to keep this party going and meet the work that inspired and informed this book, it would be a great pleasure to see you in personal coaching alongside me. Either way, having discovered real gold within, by now you are no longer in your gilded cage.

Congratulations. You are out of the Inferno. You are free.

ABOUT THE AUTHOR

A THOUGHT LEADER in the coaching world, Keren Eldad ("Coach Keren") specializes in taking high achievers out of the futility of constant pursuit and into the greatest levels of success and fulfillment. Her coaching clients include Olympic athletes, politicians, Hollywood stars, supermodels, Special Forces operatives, and serial entrepreneurs, as well as renowned global organizations such as Estée Lauder, J.P. Morgan, and Nike. She is also the founder of THE CLUB, a community of leaders, entrepreneurs, and coaches who encourage and support each other to reach their fullest potential and to make their greatest contribution.

Recognized as a Top Ten Executive Coach by the International Coaching Federation (ICF), Real Leaders Magazine, & Goop, Keren maintains gold-standard coaching credentials on top of her advanced academic degrees from the London School of Economics and the University of Jerusalem. She is also a former C-suite executive, who has lived and worked in 17 countries and on four continents and now coaches leaders all around the globe in four languages: English, Spanish, Hebrew, and French. With half a million views on her TEDx talks and speaking engagements all over the world, Keren's message seems to transcend borders. She hopes it resonates with you.

Coach Keren resides in Austin, Texas, with her husband, Ryan, and many beloved pets. For booking and coaching consultations, contact Lee@KerenEldad.com.

Mango Publishing, established in 2014, publishes an eclectic list of books by diverse authors—both new and established voices—on topics ranging from business, personal growth, women's empowerment, LGBTQ studies, health, and spirituality to history, popular culture, time management, decluttering, lifestyle, mental wellness, aging, and sustainable living. We were named 2019 *and* 2020's #1 fastest growing independent publisher by *Publishers Weekly*. Our success is driven by our main goal, which is to publish high-quality books that will entertain readers as well as make a positive difference in their lives.

Our readers are our most important resource; we value your input, suggestions, and ideas. We'd love to hear from you—after all, we are publishing books for you!

Please stay in touch with us and follow us at:

Facebook: Mango Publishing
Twitter: @MangoPublishing
Instagram: @MangoPublishing
LinkedIn: Mango Publishing
Pinterest: Mango Publishing
Newsletter: mangopublishinggroup.com/newsletter

Join us on Mango's journey to reinvent publishing, one book at a time.

www.ingramcontent.com/pod-product-compliance
Lightning Source LLC
Jackson TN
JSHW080719060125
73760JS00006BC/6